Le stime degli obiettivi fotografici
Stefano Benedetti - © 2015 – All rights reserved

Introduzione	pagina 6
Abbreviazioni	pagina 9
Acall	pagina 15
Agfa	pagina 15
Aicar	pagina 15
Albinar	pagina 16
Amar	pagina 16
Angénieux	pagina 16
Arco	pagina 17
Astro Berlin	pagina 17
Astro-Kino	pagina 19
Avanar	pagina 19
Beaud & Wallon	pagina 19
Bell & Howell	pagina 19
Beroflex	pagina 19
Boyer	pagina 20
Bower	pagina 20
C.P.Goerz	pagina 20
Canon	pagina 21
Caspeco	pagina 22
Chinon	pagina 23
Clubman	pagina 23
Dallmeyer	pagina 23
Danubigon	pagina 25
Delft and Old Delft	pagina 25
Durst	pagina 26
Edixar	pagina 26
Elbex	pagina 26
Exakta	pagina 27
Fuji	pagina 27
Hanimex	pagina 28
Hasselblad	pagina 29

Helios	pagina 29
Hoya	pagina 30
Iff	pagina 30
Industar	pagina 30
Isco	pagina 31
Itorex	pagina 31
Janpol	pagina 32
Jupiter	pagina 32
Kalimar	pagina 32
Kiev	pagina 33
Kilfitt	pagina 33
Kiron	pagina 34
Kodak	pagina 34
Komura (Sankyō Kōki K.K.)	pagina 36
Konica	pagina 37
Konica-Minolta	pagina 38
Koristka	pagina 38
Krasnogorsk	pagina 38
Kyoei	pagina 39
Lerebours & Secretan	pagina 39
Lancaster & Son	pagina 39
Leica	pagina 39
Lentar	pagina 41
Lomo	pagina 42
Makinon	pagina 43
Mamya	pagina 44
Marexar	pagina 45
Matar	pagina 45
Meopta	pagina 45
Meyer	pagina 46
Mikar	pagina 47
Minolta	pagina 47
Mir	pagina 49

Miranda	pagina 50
Mitakon	pagina 50
Naigon	pagina 51
Nicola Perscheid	pagina 51
Nikon	pagina 51
Nikula	pagina 53
Novoflex	pagina 54
Norisstar	pagina 54
Ocean	pagina 54
Officine Galileo	pagina 54
Olympus	pagina 55
Optomax	pagina 56
Osawa	pagina 56
Panagor	pagina 56
Panasonic	pagina 57
Peleng	pagina 57
Pentacon	pagina 58
Pentax	pagina 58
Petzval	pagina 60
Phokinar	pagina 60
Porst	pagina 60
Polaroid	pagina 61
Prinzflex	pagina 61
Revuenon	pagina 62
Rodenstock	pagina 63
Roeschlein Kreuznach	pagina 64
Rollei	pagina 65
Samyang	pagina 66
Schast	pagina 66
Schneider	pagina 67
Schneider –Kreusnach	pagina 68
Schulze & Billerbeck	pagina 69
Seimar	pagina 69

Sesnon	pagina 70
Sigma	pagina 70
Sinar	pagina 72
Sirius	pagina 72
Società Anonima Ambrosio	pagina 73
Soligor	pagina 73
Som Berthiot -	pagina 74
Sony	pagina 75
Staeble	pagina 78
Super Ozeck	pagina 78
Takumar	pagina 78
Tamron	pagina 80
Taylor & Hobson	pagina 82
Tefnon	pagina 82
Tiny Steinheil Cassar	pagina 83
Tokina	pagina 83
Vega	pagina 83
Vivitar	pagina 84
Voigtlander	pagina 84
Voigtlander & Sohn	pagina 85
Volna	pagina 86
Xarkov	pagina 86
Yashica	pagina 86
Yvar	pagina 87
Will Wetzlar	pagina 87
Wollensak	pagina 88
Zeiss e Carl Zeiss	pagina 88
Zenitar	pagina 90
Zenith	pagina 90
Zenza Bronica	pagina 91
Altri lavori pubblicati dall'autore	pagina 92
Chi distribuisce i libri	pagina 106
Contatta l'autore	pagina 108

Introduzione

Questo libro è frutto di una ricerca lunga e complessa effettuata in Italia, Europa e America. Abbiamo raccolto milioni di dati e poi li abbiamo elaborati con programmi creati apposta. L'obiettivo era riuscire a fornire al collezionista, al venditore, all'antiquario e al rivenditore, una valida indicazione del valore di un obiettivo fotografico usato o antico. Quello che forniamo, per ogni obiettivo, è un valore espresso con un intervallo che va dal minimo al massimo riscontrato sul mercato. I minimi e i massimi sono medie ragionate. Questo significa che il valore cercato è quello per un obiettivo funzionante non eccessivamente deteriorato. Non abbiamo preso in considerazioni offerte che corrispondevano a obiettivi fotografici in condizioni di conservazione pessime o comunque talmente deteriorati da risultare non utilizzabili. Le stime riportate nel libro sono condizionate, oltre che dallo stato di conservazione, anche dal tipo di innesto di cui è dotato l'obiettivo perché in molti casi ciò determina una variazione di prezzo rilevante. Ovviamente le stime non sono personalizzate. Qui non trovate la valutazione del vostro obiettivo fotografico, ma una stima che si riferisce ad un obiettivo fotografico uguale al vostro. Soltanto voi conoscete il reale stato di conservazione del vostro obiettivo fotografico e quindi soltanto voi potete decidere se il suo valore è più vicino alla minima quotazione o alla massima. Per questo motivo non possiamo assumerci alcuna responsabilità che potrebbe derivare dall'uso di questo libro.

Il libro è organizzato in tabelle dove possono comparire, insieme ad altre informazioni, anche delle abbreviazioni.

Riportiamo all'inizio del libro l'elenco delle abbreviazioni usate e il loro significato. Le abbreviazioni usate sono normalmente utilizzate sia dai produttori che dai fotografi. Riportiamo anche abbreviazioni usate da una marca specifica affinché l'identificazione dell'obiettivo fotografico sia certa.

Le tabelle contenenti i dati sono suddivise per produttore e questi ordinati alfabeticamente dalla A alla Z.

Dall'indice potete accedere direttamente alla marca che vi interessa.

Ogni tabella ha cinque colonne.

Nella prima colonna sono riportati il modello dell'obiettivo e qualunque informazione che possa permettere la sua identificazione. Se compare l'anno significa che la valutazione è riferita al modello prodotto in quel periodo.

Nella seconda colonna è riportata la lunghezza focale dell'obiettivo fotografico. Se compare un solo numero significa che l'obiettivo fotografico è del tipo con focale fissa e il valore è quello indicato. Se compaiono due numeri significa che la lunghezza focale è variabile (zoom). La lunghezza focale è espressa in millimetri. Nella terza colonna è indicata la luminosità massima dell'obiettivo fotografico espressa con i numeri standard internazionali f. Tanto più è grande questo numero tanto è minore la luminosità dell'obiettivo. Nella quarta colonna è indicato il tipo di innesto che connette l'obiettivo alla fotocamera.

Riportiamo all'inizio l'elenco dei tipi di innesto più comuni e il loro significato. Nell'ultima colonna è riportata la valutazione espressa in Euro. La valutazione è sempre composta da due numeri e indica l'oscillazione riscontrata tra le valutazioni attendibili esaminate.

Le stime degli obiettivi

Abbreviazioni
Qualsiasi obiettivo fotografico

Af = autofocus

Anast. = anastigmatico

Apo = lenti apocromatiche

Anam = lenti anamorfiche

As = lenti asferiche

Lf = grande formato

Pe = ingranditore fotografico

Macro = obiettivo per macrofotografia

Mc = multi coating

Mf = fuoco manuale

Canon

Do = diffractive optics

Ef = indica la compatibilità solo con il formato Full-Frame o Aps-C.

Ef-S = indica la compatibilità solo con il formato Aps-C.

Emd = electro magnetic diaphragm

Is = stabilizzatore d'immagine

L = lusso

Macro = obiettivo per macrofotografia

Numero Romano (tipo I, II, III…) = il numero romano indica la versione

Stm = stepping motor technology

Ts-E = tilt & shift

Usm = ultrasonic motor

Nikon

Af = autofocus.

Af-D = autofocus + distanza del soggetto dalla fotocamera

Af-S = autofocus + silent wave motor

Asp = lenti asferiche

Crc = Close Range Correction

Dc = defocus control

D = distanza (l'obiettivo provvede alle informazioni sulla distanza)

Dx = obiettivi dedicati a fotocamere con sensore Aps-C

Ed = extra low dispersion

G = senza ghiera dell'apertura del diaframma

If = internal focus

Pc = obiettivo decentrabile

Pf = con il componente Phase Fresnel

Rd = rear focusing

Sic = super integrated coating

Swm = silent wave motor

Vr = riduttore di vibrazioni

Pentax

Al = lenti asferiche

Da = compatibile con il sensore Aps-C

D-Fa = compatibile con il sensore Full-Frame

Ed = extra low dispersion

Fa = compatibile con il sensore Full-Frame e ghiera aperture.

If = internal

Smc = super multi-coating

Sdm = obiettivo con motore ultrasonico

Wr = resistente agli agenti atmosferici

Sigma

A = arte

Apo = lenti apocromatiche

Asp = lenti asferiche

C = contemporaneo

Conv = utilizzabile con moltiplicatore Sigmat e termicamente stabile

Dc = compatibile con il sensore Aps-C

Dg = compatibile con il sensore Full-Frame

Exx = indica un obiettivo di qualità professionale

Hsm = hyper-sonic motor

If = internal focus

Os = stabilizzatore ottico

Rf = rear focus

S = sport

Sony

G = serie professionale

M = obiettivo per macrofotografia

Sal = indica obiettivi adatti al sistema Sony Alpha

Ssm = obiettivo con motore di messa a fuoco a ultrasuoni

Stf = simile a Dc della Nikon

Z = obiettivi prodotti da Zeiss

Tamron

Ad = anomalous dispersion

Af = autofocus

Asl = lenti asferiche

Di = digitally integrated design

Di-Ii = digitally integrated design + compatibilità solo con Aps-C.

Fec = filter effect control

If = internal focusing

Ld = low dispersion.

Pzd = piezo drive

Sp = super performance

Usd = ultrasonic silent drive

Vc = compensazione delle vibrazioni

Xr = extra refractive index glass

Tokina Camera Lenses

At- X = advance technology extra

At – X Pro = advance technology extra professional

As = obiettivo asferico

Fc = focus clutch mechanism

Fe = floating element system

If = internal focus system

Mc = multi-coating

Sd = super low dispersion.

Zeiss Camera Lenses

T* = obiettivo con strati antiriflesso tipo T*

Za = Autofocus per Sony Alpha

Ze = obiettivi con messa a fuoco manuale per Canon

Zf = obiettivi con messa a fuoco manuale per Nikon

Zk = obiettivi con messa a fuoco manuale per Pentax K

Zm = obiettivi con messa a fuoco manuale per Zeiss Ikon

Zs = obiettivi con messa a fuoco manuale attacco M42

Abbreviazioni Speciali

Ar o Ar Mount o Konica Ar = attacco a baionetta introdotto da Konica

D o D Mount = filettatura di15,88 mm

F o F Mount o Nikon F = tipo di baionetta creata per le fotocamere Nikon o per obiettivi compatibili

F o F Mount o Konica F Mount = non è uguale all'attacco

Nikon F, questa baionetta ha un diametro di 40 mm.

M Mount o Leica M Mount = è un tipo di baionetta introdotto dalla Leica con un diametro di 44 mm

M37 = passo a vite di 37 mm di diametro e con un passo di 1 mm

M39 = passo a vite di 39 mm di diametro e con un passo di 1 mm

M42 = passo a vite di 42 mm di diametro e con un passo di 1 mm

Pl o Pl = Baionetta sviluppata da Arri

Projector = se trovate questa indicazione significa che l'obiettivo è stato fatto per essere usato sui proiettori (solitamente di diapositive)

R Mount o Leica R Mount = è un tipo di baionetta introdotta dalla Leica con flangia di 47 mm

T2 = passo a vite di 42 mm (draw = 55 mm)

Acall

Modello	Focale	f	Attacco	€
Acall	135	3,5	Exacta	140-180
Acall	80	----	----	50-70

Agfa

Modello	Focale	f	Attacco	€
Agfa Color Ambion	35	4	----	25-40
Agfa Color Mc	50	1,4	----	70-120
Agfa Color Solinar	50	2,8	----	20-40
Agfa Color Telinar	135	4	----	70-100
Agfa Color Telinar	90	4	----	70-100
Agfa Magnolar	80	5,6	F	45-70
Agfa Ocellar	50	----	Projector	30-45
Agfa Repromaster	213	9,25	----	55-100
Agfa Repromaster	240	9,5	----	100-150
Agfa Super Intergon	305	9	Lf	110-150
Agfa Trilinear	103	6,3	----	25-45
Agfa Variostar	6-60	1,8	----	30-60

Aicar

Modello	Focale	f	Attacco	€
Aicar	135	2,8	Canon	40-80
Aicar Auto Mc	80-205	4,5	Pentax Pk	28-50

Albinar

Modello	Focale	f	Attacco	€
Albinar	500	8	----	70-110
Albinar Macro	75-300	5,6	Contax	28-45
Albinar Mc	28	2,8	Contax	28-45
Albinar Mf	28-50	3,5-4,5	Pentax	20-40
Albinar Sc	85-200	4	Pentax	25-50
Super Albinar	75-205	4	Minolta	25-45
Super Albinar	35-75	3,5-4,8	----	35-60
Super Albinar	75-150	3,8	Minolta	25-40
Super Albinar Auto	135	3,5	----	40-55
Super Albinar Mc	80-200	3,8	Pentax	29-45
Super Albinar Mc	75-300	5,6	Contax	25-50

Amar

Modello	Focale	f	Attacco	€
Amar	55	----	----	40-60
Amar	105	4,5	----	28-50
Amar	55	4,5	M42	20-40

Angénieux

Modello	Focale	f	Attacco	€
Angenieux	70/210	3,5	Nikon	500-700
Angenieux	17-68	2,2	C	200-280
Angenieux	10-150	2-2,8	----	80-120
Angenieux	20-120	----	Arriflex	4000-5000
Angenieux	35-70	2,5-3,3	Leica R	800-1000

Angénieux	10-150	2-2,8	----	160-240
Angénieux	12-120	2,2	----	140-180
Angénieux	12-120	2,2	CPR	600-800
Angénieux	25-250	3,5	Nikon	3500-4500
Angénieux	35	3,5	M39	2800-3600
Angenieux Anast.	100	4,5	----	70-110
Angénieux Macro	70-210	3,5	Leica R	800-1000
Angenieux Retrofocus	10	1,8	C	50-80
Angénieux Type P1	90	1,8	M39	6500-8000
Angénieux Type S21	50	1,5	Exakta	8000-10000

Arco

Modello	Focale	f	Attacco	€
Arco	135	3,8	Leica	35-60
Arco Cine	65	1,4	D	45-70
Cine	13	1,8	---	20-40
Cine S	13	1,4	D	20-40
Cine T	38	1,4	---	45-85
Colinar	135	3,8	M39	70-100
Tele Colinar	135	3,5	Exc	40-70

Astro Berlin

Modello	Focale	f	Attacco	€
Askania	900	4,5	----	1000-1200
Astan	135	3,5	M39	900-1200

Astro Astran (prototipo)	47	2,9	----	400-600
Fernbildlinse	150	5	C	180-240
Fernbildlinse	300	5	Arriflex	150-220
Fernbildlinse	300	5	M39	450-550
Fernbildlinse	300	5	Contax	400-450
Fernbildlinse	400	5	M39	750-850
Fernbildlinse	1000	6,3	C	2200-2600
Gauss-Tachar	100	2	----	1500-1800
Kino VII	85	1,4	M39	5000-6000
Military	180	2,3	M39	1400-1900
Pan-Tachar	50	2,3	Leica M	600-800
Pan-Tachar	75	1,8	----	1200-1600
Pan-Tachar	75	2,3	Contax	800-1000
Pan-Tachar	100	1,8	----	1700-2000
Pan-Tachar	100	2,3	M39	1200-1500
Pan-Tachar	150	1,8	----	1200-1400
Pan-Tachar	150	2,3	----	800-1000
Pan-Tachar	150	2,3	----	1200-1400
Pan-Tachar	200	2,3	----	900-1200
Pan-Tachar	300	4,5	----	450-550
Portrait	150	2,3	M39	1800-2400
Tachar	75	2,3	M39	700-900
Tachon	35	0,95	C	550-700
Tasman	140	1,5	----	4200-4800
Telastan	500	3,5	C	400-450
Tv Tachar (cine)	50	1,5	----	2600-2900

Astro-Kino

Modello	Focale	f	Attacco	€
Astro-Kino VII	85	1,4	Canon	2000-2500
Color IV	50	1,4	----	80-120

Avanar

Modello	Focale	f	Attacco	€
Avanar Mc	28	2,8	Yashica	30-45

Beaud & Wallon

Modello	Focale	f	Attacco	€
Petzval lens for daguerrotype	----	----	----	1500-2000

Bell & Howell

Modello	Focale	f	Attacco	€
Bell & Howell	50	2	Projector	20-40
Bell & Howell	64	1,6	Projector	40-60
Filmovara	----	----	Projector	30-50
Macro	85-300	5	----	20-40
Super D Proval	48	1,4	----	20-40

Beroflex

Modello	Focale	f	Attacco	€
Auto Mc Macro	75-200	4,5	Minolta	32-55
Beroflex	35-70	3,5-4,5	Praktica	29-50
Mc Pb	80-200	3,9	Praktica	25-45

Boyer

Modello	Focale	f	Attacco	€
Jada	60	1,6	----	3000-4000
Paris B Saphir	50	3,5	----	210-280
Paris Beryl	135	6,8	----	200-260
Paris Saphir	190	4,5	----	50-70
Paris Saphir	110	4,5	----	180-220
Paris Saphir	210	4,5	----	160-200
Paris Saphir Apo	300	9	----	800-1000
Paris Saphir B	75	3,5	----	170-200
Paris Saphir BX	135	5,6	----	140-190
Paris Saphir Color	135	4,5	----	300-360
Saphir	25	2,8	----	700-800
Saphir	32	3,5	----	170-200
Saphir	300	4,5	----	350-400
Saphir Apo	135	10	----	300-380
Topaz Paris	105	4,5	----	40-65
Topaz Paris	90	4,5	----	250-290

Bower

Modello	Focale	f	Attacco	€
Bower	650-1300	8	Canon Eos	160-220
Bower Mc	28	2,8	----	20-50
Bower MF	500	8	Nikon	120-180
Bower Sly	8	3,5	Nikon	140-180

C.P.Goerz

Modello	Focale	f	Attacco	€
Dagor	100	9	----	500-600
Dagor	24	2,8	----	180-250
Dagor Anast	180	6,8	----	300-360
Dagor Anast	120	6,8	----	800-950
Dogmar (1920)	150	4,5	----	280-400

Hypergon Doppel Anastigmat	----	----	----	1800-2500
Serie Ib Celor Anast	240	5	----	55-80
Tenastigmat	130	6,8	----	29-45

Canon

Modello	Focale	f	Attacco	€
Canon	50	0,95	Leica M	2000-2400
Canon	50	1,5	Canon	400-600
Canon	50	1,8	Canon	180-280
Canon	50	2,8	Canon	150-250
Canon	35-70	3,5-4,5	Canon	80-120
Canon	80-200	4	Canon	80-100
Canon (1953)	100	3,5	Canon	180-290
Canon (1959)	100	2	Canon	450-700
Canon Fd	200	4	Canon	70-100
Canon (1951)	85	1,9	Canon	200-400
Canon (1952)	85	1,5	Canon	400-600
Canon (1956)	25	3,5	Canon	400-600
Canon (1956)	50	1,2	Canon	400-700
Canon (1957)	28	2,8	Canon	280-480
Canon (1957)	35	1,8	Canon	300-480
Canon (1957)	50	1,4	Canon	350-450
Canon (1958)	35	1,5	Canon	500-800
Canon (1961)	50	0,95	Canon	1000-1600
Canon (1961)	85	1,8	Canon	550-800
Canon (1962)	35	2	Canon	400-600
Canon nera(1956)	50	1,2	Canon	700-900
Canon Ef	100-400	4,5-5,6	Canon	650-800
Canon Ef	38-76	4,5-5,6	Canon	40-70
Canon Ef	35-80	4-5,6	Canon	40-70
Canon Ef	18-55	3,5-5,6	Canon	80-110

Canon Ef	18-55	3,5-5,6	Canon	80-110
Canon Ef	18-135	3,5-5,6	Canon	200-250
Canon Ef	50	1,8	Canon	70-120
Canon Ef Usm	50	1,4	Canon	400-550
Canon Ef-S Stm	18-135	3,5-5,6	Canon	450-550
Canon Fd	24	2	Canon	200-280
Canon Fd	135	3,5	Canon	45-65
Canon Fd	300	5,6	Canon	90-120
Canon Fd	35-105	3,5	Canon	80-100
Canon Fd	50	1,8	Canon	60-85
Canon Fd	70-210	4	Canon	70-100
Canon Mf	50-135	3,5	Canon	85-125
Canon Serenar	50	1,9	Canon	180-280
Canon Serenar (1948)	135	4	Canon	80-120
Canon Serenar (1948)	85	2	Canon	200-300
Canon Serenar (1948)	100	4	Canon	80-120
Canon Serenar (1951)	35	2,8	Canon	200-280
Canon Serenar (1951)	28	3,5	Canon	220-400
Canon Serenar (1951)	35	3,2	Canon	200-280
Canon Serenar (1952)	135	3,5	Canon	80-120
Canon Serenar (1952)	50	3,5	Canon	250-400

Caspeco

Modello	Focale	f	Attacco	€
Caspeco	135	2,8	----	30-50
Caspeco	28	3,5	T/T2	40-70
Caspeco Auto	35	2,8	----	20-40
Caspeco Auto Tele	135	3,5	Ai	45-60

Chinon

Modello	Focale	f	Attacco	€
Chinon	200	3.5	----	60-90
Chinon	135	2,8	----	68-88
Chinon	55	1,7	M42	25-45
Chinon Af	28-70	3.5-4.5	---	20-40
Chinon Af	70-210	4,5	----	30-60
Chinon Auto	28	3,5	M42	25-45
Chinon Auto	50	1,4	----	27-40
Chinon Auto	35	2,8	----	20-40
Chinon Auto	135	2,8	Canon Ef	25-40
Chinon Auto	50	1,9	Pentax K	22-40
Chinon Auto	55	1,4	M42	80-120
Chinon Macro Mc	55	1,7	M42	100-150
Chinon Mc	28-50	3,5-4,5	Pentax	25-50

Clubman

Modello	Focale	f	Attacco	€
Clubman	80-200	4,5-5,6	M42	20-30

Dallmeyer

Modello	Focale	f	Attacco	€
Adon (alluminio e ottone)	----	1	----	150-190
Dallmeyer	12	3,5	----	100-140
Dallmeyer	6,5	2,5	D	75-110

Dallmeyer	82	4	C	250-310
Dallmeyer	25	1,9	C	400-500
Dallmeyer	175	----	Projector	140-180
Dallmeyer	74	----	Projector	80-120
Dallmeyer	50	----	Projector	45-75
Dallmeyer Anast	300	3,5	----	900-1200
Dallmeyer Anast	12	6,5	----	90-140
Dallmeyer Anast	20	3,5	C	160-190
Dallmeyer Anast	152	5,6	39	400-500
Dallmeyer Anast	13	1,9	D	120-160
Dallmeyer Anast	135	4,5	----	220-300
Dallmeyer Anast	76	4,5	----	160-190
Dallmeyer Anast	133	6,5	----	340-400
Dallmeyer Anast	178	5,6	----	180-240
Dallmeyer Pentac	190	2,9	----	100-140
Dallmeyer Series VI	280	4,5	----	140-180
Dallon	230	6,5	----	350-470
Dallon Anast	150	5,6	M39	400-500
Military	12	3,5	----	250-360
Rapide Landascape N°2	280	6,3	----	320-370
Rapide Landascape N°4	330	16	----	400-500
Rapide Landascape N°4	550	11	----	700-800
Soft focus	152	4,5	----	950-1200
Speed Anast	20	1,5	----	500-600
Stigmatic	381	6	----	500-600
Super Anast	50	2	Leica	14000-16000

Super Six	63	1,9	----	14000-16000
Super six Anast	24	1,9	----	1400-1800
Triple Anast	24	2,9	C	550-650

Danubigon

Modello	Focale	f	Attacco	€
Auto Mc	28-70	3-4,5	Olymous Om	20-40
Danubigon	80-200	4	Minolta Md	20-40
Danubigon	135	2,8	----	20-40
Danubigon	35-70	3,5-4,5	Minolta	25-45
Danubigon Auto	28-70	3-4,5	Olympus	25-45

Delft and Old Delft

Modello	Focale	f	Attacco	€
Aereo Jet	305	4	----	500-600
Alefar	180	4,5	Alpa	240-280
Alpa Alefar	180	4,5	----	200-240
De Oude	400	6,3	----	60-90
De Oude	100	1,4	----	1400-1700
Delca	50	6,3	Minolta	1400-1600
Delca	500	6,3	Contax	3500-4500
Delca T.C.	2000	14	----	1500-2500
Delfar	90	4,5	Leica	1400-1600
Delft	400	5	----	800-1000

Delft	35	3,5	----	900-1100
Delft Alpa (Prototype)	37	3,5	----	1500-1800
Deltamar	150	2,8	----	450-550
Fototel	400	4,5	Exakta	700-850
Fototel	450	5,6	M39	800-1000
Minor	37	3,5	Alpa	1400-1800
Minor (Prototipo)	37	3,5	Alpa	900-1200
Rayxar	50	0,75	----	900-1200

Durst

Modello	Focale	f	Attacco	€
Comparon	50	4	----	40-60
Componon	150	5,6	----	120-170
Mitub	39	1	Pe	25-45
Neonon	80	5,6	Pe	20-40
Netaron	50	2,8	Pe	28-45

Edixar

Modello	Focale	f	Attacco	€
Edixar	95-205	6,3	M42	45-80
Edixar	85-210	4,8	M42	48-70
Edixar	135	2,8	M42	29-45
Edixar	28	2,8	M42	29-45

Elbex

Modello	Focale	f	Attacco	€
Tv lens	8	1,3	----	55-80

Exakta

Modello	Focale	f	Attacco	€
Exakta	500	8	Canon	80-120
Exakta	35-80	4-5,6	Minolta	40-60
Exakta	80	2,8	----	250-350
Exakta	35-100	3,5-4,5	----	70-90
Exakta	54	3,5	----	450-550
Exakta macro	28-70	4	----	25-55
Exakta Mc macro	70-210	4,5-5,6	----	45-70

Fuji

Modello	Focale	f	Attacco	€
Fujinon	50	1,9	----	40-60
Fujinon A	180	9	----	655-795
Fujinon A	240	9	----	680-820
Fujinon C	300	8,5	----	655-795
Fujinon C	450	12,5	----	925-1065
Fujinon C	600	11,5	----	1525-1665
Fujinon Cm-W	105	5,6	----	575-715
Fujinon Cm-W	125	5,6	----	575-715
Fujinon Cm-W	135	5,6	----	625-765
Fujinon Cm-W	150	5,6	----	625-765
Fujinon Cm-W	180	5,6	----	725-865
Fujinon Cm-W	210	5,6	----	805-945
Fujinon Cm-W	250	6,3	----	905-1045
Fujinon Cm-W	300	5,6	----	1525-1665
Fujinon Cm-W	360	6,5	----	1855-1995

Fujinon Cm-W	450	8	----	2155-2295
Fujinon Sw	90	8	----	725-865
Fujinon Sw	105	8	----	1125-1265
Fujinon Sw	125	8	----	1125-1265
Fujinon Swd	65	5,6	----	1025-1165
Fujinon Swd	75	5,6	----	1155-1295
Fujinon Swd	90	5,6	----	1225-1365
Fujinon T	300	8	----	780-920
Fujinon T	400	8	----	1025-1165
Fujinon T	600	12	----	1525-1665

Hanimex

Modello	Focale	f	Attacco	€
Hanimex	80-200	4.5	M42	25-45
Hanimex	90-210	4	----	45-70
Hanimex	102	2,8	----	50-75
Hanimex	500	8	----	70-110
Hanimex	200	4,5	M42	30-55
Hanimex	35-75	3,5-4,5	----	40-60
Hanimex	600	8	Nikon	120-160
Hanimex Auto	70-140	3,8	Minolta Md	26-45
Hanimex Auto	28-80	5,6	Minolta Md	28-45
Hanimex Auto Mf	35	2.8	M42	80-100
Hanimex Macro Auto	75-300	5,6	----	25-45
Hanimex Mc	28	2,8	Konica	28-45
Hanimex Mc Auto	135	2,8	----	40-70

Hasselblad

Modello	Focale	f	Attacco	€
Distagon	40	4	----	900-1000
Hasselblad 2000	60-120	4,8	----	600-700
Hasselblad 2000	50	2,8	----	1600-1900
Hasselblad Cb	120	4	----	2000-2500
Hasselblad Cf	180	4	----	2500-3500
Hasselblad Cf	500	8	----	5000-6000
Hasselblad Cf	100	3.5	----	2000-2800
Hasselblad Cf	150	4	----	400-460

Helios

Modello	Focale	f	Attacco	€
Helios 40	85	1,5	Nikon	400-450
Helios 40	85	1,5	Micro 4/3	380-420
Helios 40	85	1,5	Sony NEX	400-450
Helios 40	85	1,5	Samsung Nx	400-420
Helios 40	85	1,5	Canon FD	400-450
Helios 40	85	1,5	Contax / Yashica	420-460
Helios 44-2	58	2	Samsung NX	50-90
Helios 44	58	2	Zenit	40-70
Helios 44 argento	58	2	M39	80-160
Helios 44M	58	2	Nikon	60-90
Helios 77M	50	1,8	Nikon	120-160

Hoya

Modello	Focale	f	Attacco	€
Hoya Hmc	28-85	4	Contax	20-35
Hoya Hmc	100-300	5,6	Pentax	25-40
Hoya Hmc	80-200	4	Olympus	25-40
Hoya Hmc	70-150	3,8	Pentax	30-55
Hoya Hmc	135	2,8	Contax	40-60
Hoya Hmc Macro	35-105	4	Olympus	30-50

Iff

Modello	Focale	f	Attacco	€
Dugor	50	4,5	----	40-70

Industar

Modello	Focale	f	Attacco	€
Industar	50	3,5	M39	15-28
Industar	55	2,8	M39	28-45
Industar	50	2,8	M42	80-120
Industar	80	2,8	----	70-100
Industar	110	4,5	Pe M39	22-40
Industar	28	2,8	M39	28-40
Industar	50	2	M42	25-40
Industar	53	2,8	M39	22-35
Industar 4 (1938)	210	4,5	----	180-240
Industar	50	3,5	Nikon	29-50
Industar	50	3,5	Olympus 4/3	30-60
Industar-61 L/Z	50	2,8	Nikon	60-85
Industar-61 L/Z	50	2,8	Olympus 4/3	55-80
Macro	105	3,5	----	85-140

Isco

Modello	Focale	f	Attacco	€
Isco Gottingen Isconar	135	4	Exakta	15-28
Isco Göttingen Vario Stellar	85-150	3,5	Projector	90-120
Isco Optic Blue Star Ultra	70	----	Projector	60-90
Isco Optic Ultra	95	2	Projector	60-85
Isco Red Ultra Star HD Plus	75	2,4	Projector	100-140
Isco Red Ultra Star HD Plus	85	2.4	Projector	90-140
Isco Super-Kiptar	70	2	Projector	60-90
Isco-Gottingen Cinelux	85	2	Projector	85-145
Isco-Gottingen Isconar	100	4	M42	50-80
Isco-Gottingen Projar	200	3,5	Projector	45-70
Isco-Gottingen Westanar	135	3,5	M42	55-95
Isco-Gottingen Westanar	50	2,8	M42	45-70
Isco-Gottingen Westrocolor	50	1,9	Exakta	60-90
Isco-Optic Ultra-Star	55	---	----	60-100

Itorex

Modello	Focale	f	Attacco	€
Itorex	80-200	4,5-5,2	M42	28-45
Itorex auto	80-200	5,5	----	50-80
Itorex Mc	35-135	3,9-5,3	----	20-40
Itorex Mc auto	38-70	3,5	----	45-85
Itorex Pk	28	2,8	Pentax	50-80

Janpol

Modello	Focale	f	Attacco	€
Janpol Color	80	5,6	Pe	28-45
Janpol Color K	55	5,6	Pe	28-45
Janpol Color K	90	5,6	Pe	28-45

Jupiter

Modello	Focale	f	Attacco	€
Jupiter	135	2,8	M42	35-55
Jupiter (1958) argento	50	2	M39	20-45
Jupiter 3 (1961)	50	1,5	Leica	110-140
Jupiter 3 (1955)	50	1,5	Contax	160-200
Jupiter-37	135	3,5	Olympus 4/3	110-150
Jupiter 8	50	2	M39	30-45
Jupiter 9	85	2	Arriflex	150-250
Jupiter 9	85	2	Olympus 4/3	180-220
Jupiter 9	85	2	Samsung Nx	180-220
Jupiter 9	85	2	Nikon	130-150
Jupiter 11	135	4	M39	35-55
Jupiter 12	35	2,8	M39	40-60
Jupiter 21m	200	4	M42	38-60
Jupiter 37	135	3,5	Olympus 4/3	110-150

Kalimar

Modello	Focale	f	Attacco	€
Kalimar	50	2,8	Minolta	25-45
Kalimar a specchio	500	8	T2	40-65
Kalimar auto	80-200	4,5-5,6	Canon Fd	30-50
Kalimar auto	135	2,8	Konica	40-60

Kalimar auto macro	60-300	4-5,6	Minolta	20-40
Kalimar macro	28	2,8	Pentax	35-55
Kalimar Mc	50	1,7	Contax	25-45
Kalimar Mc Af	28-200	3,5-5,6	Minolta	40-65
Kalimar Mc Af macro	70-210	3,9	----	25-45
Kalimar Mc auto	28-70	3,9-4,8	Ar	25-45

Kiev

Modello	Focale	f	Attacco	€
Kiev	80	2,8	Kiev	50-80
Telear-5	250	5,6	----	45-70
Vega 11Y	50	2,8	M39	25-45
Vega 7	20	2	----	110-160
Vega 9	50	2,1	M39	25-45
Vega-12	90	2,8	----	55-80
Volna-3	80	2,8	----	85-120
Zodiac-8	30	3,5	Kiev 88	200-250

Kilfitt

Modello	Focale	f	Attacco	€
Fern- Kilar	400	5,6	M39	150-190
Kilar	135	3,8	----	170-220
Kilar	150	3,5	----	150-180
Kilfitt	90	3,5	M39	150-190
Macro Zoomar	50-125	4	----	140-170
Makro-Kilar	40	2,8	Alpa	170-240

Makro-Kilar	40	2,8	M42	180-220
Makro-Kilar	40	3,5	----	220-250
Makro-Kilar	90	2,8	Alpa	250-290
Pan-Tele-Kilar	300	4	Arriflex	190-240
Sport-Fern-Kilar	600	5,6	C	700-900
Sport-Zoomatar	600	5,6	Arri	250-350
Tele-Kilar	105	4	----	900-1200
Tele-Kilar	300	5,6	M39	150-190

Kiron

Modello	Focale	f	Attacco	€
Kiron	28-70	3,5-4,5	Canon	60-90
Kiron	70-210	4,5-5,6	Canon	80-120
Kiron	80-200	4	Ai-s	29-45
Kiron	28-85	2,8-3,8	Minolta Md	50-80
Kiron	28	2	Olympus Om	65-90
Kiron	30-80	3,5-4,5	Canon Fd	20-45
Kiron	28-105	3,2-4,5	Olympus Om	25-45
Kiron	35-200	3,8-5,2	Pentax	28-50
Kiron	35-135	3,5-4,5	Yashica	55-80
Kiron macro	105	2,8	Canon Fd	200-280

Kodak

Modello	Focale	f	Attacco	€
Kodak Xenon	80	4	Retina	25-55
Kodak Vario Retinar	70-200	---	---	25-55
Kodak Ektar	100	4,5	Projector	45-70
Kodak Vario Retinar	85-210	3,9	Projector	35-55
Kodak Carousel Retinar	250	----	----	25-40

Kodak Ektapro Elmo	70-210	3,5	Projector	20-45
Kodak Ektapro	100-200	3,5	Projector	20-40
Kodak Ektar Aereo	178	2,5	Aerial Camera	150-250
Kodak Retina Tele Exenar	135	4	----	40-70
Kodak Retinar	90	2,5	----	30-65
Kodak Ektar	203	7,7	ILf	140-180
Kodak Carousel	180	----	Projector	18-29
Kodak Retinar S-Av	180	----	Projector	40-60
Kodak Cine Ektanon	210	2,7	----	20-35
Kodak Retinar	150	----	Projector	20-40
Kodak Ektapro	85	2,8	Projector	20-40
Kodak Retinar S-Av2000	250		Projector	60-95
Kodak Gear	78-215	4,5-5,6	Canon Eos	60-100
Kodak Retinar S-Av2000	53	4	Projector	38-55
Kodak Ektar Con Synchro-Compur	101	4.5	----	100-160
Kodak Ff	75-120	3,5	Projector	45-60
Kodak Cine 16 Mm	76	4,5	---	28-55
Kodak Retinar S-Av 1000	85	----	Projector	40-75
Kodak Retinar S-Av 1000	150	----	----	25-45
Kodak Retina Exenar	50	2,8	----	40-70
Kodak Retinar S-Av2000	250		Projector	60-95
Kodak Gear	78-215	4,5-5,6	Canon Eos	60-100

Kodak Retinar S-Av2000	53	4	Projector	38-55
Kodak Ektar Con Synchro-Compur	101	4.5	----	100-160
Kodak Ff	75-120	3,5	Projector	45-60
Kodak Cine 16 Mm	76	4,5	---	28-55
Kodak Retinar S-Av 1000	85	----	Projector	40-75
Kodak Retinar S-Av 1000	150	----	----	25-45

Komura (Sankyō Kōki K.K.)

Modello	Focale	f	Attacco	€
Komura	200	4,5	Leica	50-85
Komura	135	2,8	M42	90-120
Komura	300	5	M39	190-220
Komura	100	1,8	M42	550-650
Komura	135	3,5	Fed - Zorki	45-70
Komura	105	3,5	M39	95-140
Komura	35	2,8	M39	180-240
Komura	400	2,8	----	90-140
Komura	105	4,5	M39	50-75
Komura	45	4,5	Bronica	250-310
Komura	200	3,5	M42	170-220
Komura	35	2,5	Miranda	100-140
Komura	24	3,5	Minolta Md	170-220
Komura	75	5,6	Pe	40-60
Komura	85	1,4	Leica R	900-1100
Komura	105	2	Leica	900-1100
Komura	105	2,3	----	400-500
Komura	28	3,5	Leica	900-1100
Komura	135	2	Nikon Slr	750-850

Komura	80	1,8	Leica	750-850
Komuranon	80-210	4,5	Nikon	50-70
Komuranon Macro	38-90	3,5	Canon	70-100
Macro	75-150	4,5	----	45-60
Sper Komura	50	3,5	Bronica	240-290

Konica

Modello	Focale	f	Attacco	€
Hexanon	135	3,5	----	35-55
Hexanon	50	1,4	----	55-80
Hexanon	135	3,2	----	45-60
Hexanon	85	1,8	Ar	270-320
Hexanon	80-200	4	Ar	60-80
Hexanon	40	1,8	----	40-60
Hexanon	50	1,8	Konica	28-40
Hexanon	50	1,7	Ar	28-40
Hexanon	200	4	Ar	45-70
Hexanon	24	2,8	----	120-150
Hexanon	52	1,8	Ar	45-70
Hexanon	35-70	4	----	40-70
Hexanon	80-200	3,5	Ar	40-70
Hexanon M	50	1,2	----	1400-1800
Hexanon Macro	35-70	3,5-4,5	Ar	55-75
Hexanon Mf	57	1,4	Ar	55-80
Hexanon Mf	50	1,8	----	28-45
Konica	28	3.5	Konica	25-45
Konica	40	1,8	Konica	25-45
Konica	35	2,8	----	80-100

Konica-Minolta

Modello	Focale	f	Attacco	€
Hexanon	21	2,8	----	1000-1200
Hexar	28	3,5	Ar	28-40
Konica Minolta	18-200	3,5-6,3	----	190-300
Konica Minolta	11-18	4,5-5,6	----	370-490
Konica Minolta	18-70	3,5-5,6	----	50-80
Konica Minolta	28-100	3,5-5,6	----	30-70
Konica Minolta	17-35	2,8-4,0	----	290-390
Konica Minolta	28-75	2,8	----	280-395
Macro	100	2,8	----	350-500
Maxxum Af	28-135	4-4,5	Sony	90-140
Maxxum Af	50	1,7	----	40-65

Koristka

Modello	Focale	f	Attacco	€
Koristka Milano	120	----	----	120-180

Krasnogorsk

Modello	Focale	f	Attacco	€
Jupiter-12	35	2,8	M39	80-120
Jupiter-6	180	2,8	M42	180-240
Orion	200	6,3	----	200-260
Russar MP	20	5,6	----	180-240
Tair	300	4,5	M39	450-550
Vega 12-B	90	2,8	Kiev	60-90
Zenit Mir-20M MC	20	3,5	M42	120-140
Zenitar-K MC	20	2,8	Pentax	140-180
Zk	50	1,5	----	160-220
Zk	50	1,5	M39	160-220

Kyoei

Modello	Focale	f	Attacco	€
Acall	35	3,5	M39	240-280
Kyoei	180	3,5	Exakta	200-250
Kyoei	135	3,5	----	70-90
Super Acall	105	3,5	Leica	80-110

Lerebours & Secretan

Modello	Focale	f	Attacco	€
Per dagherrotipia (ottone)	---	----	----	700-900

Lancaster & Son

Modello	Focale	f	Attacco	€
Rectygraph (ottone)	---	----	----	80-150

Leica

Modello	Focale	f	Attacco	€
Apo-Macro-Elmarit	100	2,8	Leica R	1000-1600
Apo-Telyt-M nero	135	3,4	Leica M	1600-2000
Elmar	35	3,5	----	180-280
Elmar	50	2,8	----	280-400
Elmar	90	4	----	120-170
Elmar	105	6,3	----	900-1200
Elmar	135	4	----	300-400
Elmar (scala rossa)	50	3,5	----	400-500
Elmar All cromato	90	4	----	1200-1400
Elmar nero	135	4,5	----	120-180
Elmar cromato	135	4,5	----	80-120

Elmar cromato (1955)	90	4	----	250-320
Elmar Coated	50	3,5	----	280-380
Elmar Uncoated cromato	50	3,5	----	180-280
Elmar Uncoated nichel	50	3,5	----	200-280
Elmari-M Asph. nero	24	3,8	Leica M	1400-1800
Elmarit	90	4	----	700-900
Elmarit	90	2,8	----	700-900
Elmarit-M	21	2,8	Leica M	1400-1600
Elmarit-M Asph.	24	2,8	Leica M	1400-1800
Elmarit-R	19	2,8	Leica R	1500-2500
Elmarit-R	135	2,8	Leica R	300-360
Elmarit-R Fish Eye	16	2,8	Leica R	600-700
Hektor	135	4,5	----	90-160
Hektor (1938)	135	4,5	M39	180-220
Hektor cromato	28	6,3	----	420-620
Hektor cromato	50	2,5	----	380-450
Hektor Coated	28	6,3	----	420-620
Hektor Nickel	28	6,3	----	480-680
Hektor Nickel	50	2,5	----	450-550
Hektor Rapid	27	1,4	C	240-280
Macro Elmar-R	100	4	Leica R	300-500
Summar nero Rim	50	2	----	180-280
Summar cromato	50	2	----	1400-2000
Summar Coated	50	2	----	250-350
Summar Nikel	50	2	----	1000-1600
Summar Uncoated	50	2	----	180-280
Summarex nero	85	1,5	----	1400-1700
Summarex cromato	85	1,5	----	900-1400
Summarit	50	1,5	----	350-550
Summaron	35	2,8	----	550-650
Summaron	35	3,5	----	320-450
Summaron	28	5,6	----	720-820
Summaron (1955)	35	3,5	----	700-800
Summicron	35	2	----	1800-2400
Summicron	50	2	----	360-480

Summicron	90	2	----	700-900
Summicron (1999)	50	2	----	1400-1800
Summicron (1999)	35	2	----	1800-3000
Summicron Rigid	50	2	----	2000-2500
Summilux	50	1,4	----	3000-4000
Summilux-M Asp nero	24	1,4	Leica M	3000-4000
Summilux-M Asp nero	21	1,4	Leica M	4000-5000
Summitar	50	2	----	250-350
Summitar (1950)	50	2	----	400-550
Super-Angulon	21	4	----	1400-1800
Super-Elmar-Asp nero	18	3,8	Leica M	1700-2000
Tele-Elmar	135	4	Leica M	350-450
Telyt-R	250	4	Leica R	240-280
Thambar	90	2,2	----	2000-4000
Xenon Chrome	50	1,5	----	450-550
Xenon Nickel	50	1,5	----	600-800

Lentar

Modello	Focale	f	Attacco	€
Lentar	135	3,5	M42	35-60
Lentar	90-230	4,5	M42	35-55
Lentar	80-200	3,5	Leicaflex R	80-110
Lentar	75	3,5	----	40-55
Lentar	200	4,5	----	75-90
Lentar	250	4,5	Rollei	70-95
Lentar	90-190	5,8	----	35-60
Lentar	75-230	4,5	M42	35-60
Lentar auto	75-210	4,5	----	25-45
Lentar auto	80	3,5	Pentax	40-70
Lentar Mf	200	3,5	Nikon Ai	60-90
Super Lentar	28	2,8	----	45-65

Super Lentar	35	2,8	M42	29-48
Super Lentar	35	2,8	Minolta	45-75
Super Lentar auto	21	3,8	----	20-50
Tele Lentar	350	5,6	M42	28-45
Tele Lentar	300	5,5	Pentax	70-100
Tele Lentar	135	2,8	Minolta Md	30-50
Tele Lentar	500	2,8	----	60-80
Tele Lentar	400	6,3	----	30-50

Lomo

Modello	Focale	f	Attacco	€
Kmz	50	2	----	70-100
Kmz	135	4	----	50-70
Loomp	75	2	----	450-550
Mc Volna	50	1,8	----	70-100
Okc Helios	35	2	Arriflex	120-160
Okc Ro3	50	2	----	120-160
Okc1	50	2	----	140-180
Okc1	18	2,8	----	160-200
Okc1	100	2	----	650-800
Okc1	35	2	----	120-160
Okc11	35	2	----	470-570
Okc14	75	1,5	----	2200-2800
Okc2	25	2,8	----	80-120
Okc3	10	1,8	Kinor	150-250
Okc4	75	2,8	----	250-350
Okc4	28	2	----	220-290
Okc8	35	2	----	150-250
Oks1	100	2,8	Pentax	550-650
Oks1	50	2	----	900-1100
Oks1	16	3	----	1900-3500

Oks1	150	2,8	----	750-900
Oks2	100	2,8	----	450-550
Oks5	18	2,5	----	140-180
Oks5	18	2,5	----	900-1100
Oks6	75	2	----	280-340
Oks6	75	2	Pl	900-1100
Oks6 Macro	75	2	----	800-1100
Oks7	28	2	----	70-100
Oks7	28	2	----	160-220
Oks8	35	2	----	70-120
Oks8	35	2	----	150-190
Pf18-1	20-120	2,5	----	4000-4500
Po504	130	2	Projector	40-70
Ro502	110	2	Projector	40-70
Ussr	----	----	Projector	45-60

Makinon

Modello	Focale	f	Attacco	€
Makinon	200	3,3	Minolta Md	25-55
Makinon	80-200	4,5	M42	25-45
Makinon	75-150	4,5	Pentax K	25-40
Makinon	28	2,8	Pentax	25-50
Makinon	80-200	3,5	Minolta	29-55
Makinon	80-200	4	Konica	25-45
Makinon auto	135	2,8	Pentax	25-50
Makinon Auto	28-80	3,5-4,5	Canon AL	25-45
Makinon auto Mc	24	2,8	Minolta Md	55-80
Makinon Auto	28-70	3,5-4,5	Minolta Md	25-45
Makinon Auto Mc	300	4	Canon FD	95-120
Makinon Macro Catadiottrico	300	5,6	Fujica	70-95
Makinon Macro Catadiottrico	300	5,6	Rollei/ Voigtl	80-120

Makinon Macro Catadiottrico	400	6,7	Fujica	100-120
Makinon Macro Catadiottrico	400	6,7	Rollei/ Voigtl	110-140
Makinon MC Macro	35-105	3,5	----	30-55
Makinon Mc reflex	500	8	Pentax	55-75

Mamya

Modello	Focale	f	Attacco	€
Apo-Sekor Z	500	6	----	1400-1800
Apo-Sekor Z	350	5,6	----	350-450
Mamiya-Sekor	37	4,5	----	400-480
Fish-eye SX Auto	14	3,5	M42	240-320
Mamiya	28	3,5	----	70-100
Mamiya ES	135	2,8	----	28-50
Mamiya Sekor	90	3,8	----	28-50
Mamiya Sekor	500	8	----	280-350
Mamiya Sekor	500	5,6	----	250-320
Mamiya Sekor	360	6	----	350-450
Mamiya Sekor	210	4	----	140-190
Mamiya Sekor	150	3,5	----	100-140
Mamiya Sekor	65	4,5	----	120-160
Mamiya Sekor C	65	4,5	----	120-160
Mamiya Sekor C	127	3,8	----	90-120
Mamiya Sekor C	55	2,8	----	150-200
Mamiya Sekor E	135	2.8	----	28-50
Mamiya Sekor E	200	4	----	28-50
Mamiya Sekor Macro C	80	4	----	170-220
Mamiya Sekor Macro Z	140	4,5	----	270-340
Mamiya Sekor Z w	127	3,5	----	190-240

Mamiya-Sekor	55	4,5	----	250-350
Mamiya-Sekor C	45	2,8	----	120-160
Mamiya-Sekor C Shift	50	4	----	260-320
Mamiya-Sekor SF	150	4	----	280-340
Mamiya-Sekor Shift Z W	75	4,5	----	550-750
Mamiya-Sekor Z	65	4	----	250-350
Mamiya-Sekor Z W	250	4,5	----	190-240
Mamiya-Sekor Z W	180	4,5	----	140-180
Mamiya-Sekor Zoom	55-100	4,5	----	180-240
Mamya-Sekor	50	1,7	----	45-65
Mamya-Sekor	50	4,5	----	160-200
Press-Sekor	250	5	----	450-550
Sekor Macro	60	2,8	M42	80-120
Uld C N	300	5,6	----	90-140

Marexar

Modello	Focale	f	Attacco	€
Marexar	80-200	4,5	Canon	45-85

Matar

Modello	Focale	f	Attacco	€
Matar	50	4,5	M42	20-35

Meopta

Modello	Focale	f	Attacco	€
Anaret	105	4,5	M39	60-90
Belar	75	4,5	C	45-80

Belar	105	4,5	M30	30-50
Belar	55	4,5	Pe	35-40
Dittar	105	3,5	Pe	60-85
Largor	12,5	1,8	M25	120-160
Meopar	210	4,5	Lf	40-70
Meopta	75	4,5	23,5	15-28
Meopta	240	5,6	Projector	35-55
Meostigmat	70	1,4	Projector	190-240
Meostigmat	100	1,7	Projector	280-340
Miron	150	2,8	Projector	55-75
Openar	80	2,8	C	90-140
Openar	20	1,5	C	75-100
Openar	20	1,8	Micro 4/3	75-120
Openar	40	1,8	C	170-220
Tele Mirar	135	4,5	M37	100-140

Meyer

Modello	Focale	f	Attacco	€
Gorlitz Primoplan	58	1.9	Exakta	200-250
Jubilee Edition	210	4,5	----	240-280
Kino-Plasmat	35	1,5	----	7000-9000
Kino-Plasmat	12,5	1,5	----	300-500
Kino-Plasmat	50	1,5	Contax	16000-24000
Kino-Plasmat	50	2	M39	480-620
Makro-Plasmat	35	2,7	M39	14000-19000

Makro-Plasmat	75	2,9	M39	1200-1600
Makro-Plasmat	105	2,7	Exakta	1900-2600
Meyer	500	5,6	Pentacon	220-280
Optik Gorlitz	30	3,5	Exakta	100-140
Domiron	50	2	Exakta	800-1000
Oreston	50	1,8	Exakta	90-140
Primoplan	75	1,9	Exakta	950-1200
Optik Trioplan	50	2,9	Exakta	80-130
Orestegon	300	4	Exakta	65-95
Primagon	35	4,5	Exakta	40-70
Primoplan	58	1,9	M39	1400-1900
Primoplan	80	1,9	Exakta	1500-2000
Primoplan	100	1,9	Exakta	1400-1900
Primotar	85	2,8	Exakta	320-400
Telemegor	400	5.5	Exakta	140-170
Telemegor	300	4,5	----	70-90
Telemegor V	400	5,5	Hasselblad	280-340
Trioplan	100	2,8	Exakta	70-100
Trioplan	105	4,5	M39	700-900
Weitwinkel Doppel Anast	40	4,5	M39	1200-1600

Mikar

Modello	Focale	f	Attacco	€
Mikar	55	4,5	Pe	20-40

Minolta

Modello	Focale	f	Attacco	€
Minolta	17-35	3,5 G	----	950-1250
Minolta	20-35	3,5-4,5	----	200-250
Minolta	24-50	4	----	100-145
Minolta	24-105	3,5-4,5	----	175-230

Minolta	28-100	3,5-5,6	----	25-80
Minolta	28-135	4-4,5	----	200-350
Minolta	35-70	4	----	25-80
Minolta	70-210	3,5-4,5	----	65-90
Minolta	100-200	4,5	----	60-100
Minolta	100-400	4,5-6,7	----	405-520
Minolta	20	2,8	----	350-425
Minolta	24	2,8	----	135-200
Minolta	28	2,8	----	50-120
Minolta	28	2	----	560-690
Minolta	35	2	----	650-850
Minolta	50	1,7	----	60-100
Minolta	50	1,4	----	175-250
Minolta	100	2	----	700-950
Minolta	135	2,8	----	250-400
Minolta Af	20	2,8	Minolta	300-360
Minolta Af	50	1,7	Minolta	100-140
Minolta Af	70-210	4	----	80-120
Minolta Af	35-80	4-5,6	----	40-60
Minolta Af Zoom	80-200	4,5-5,6	----	90-120
Minolta Apo	100-300	4,5-5,6	----	225-350
Minolta Apo	200	2,8	----	700-900
Minolta Big Beercan	75-300	4,5-5,6	----	205-300
Minolta Macro	100	2,8	----	350-500
Minolta Rokkor	200	4	Minolta	35-55
Minolta Shutter	80-200	4,5-5,6	----	35-50
Minolta (Beercan)	70-210	4	----	125-200
Minolta (D)	75-300	4,5-5,6	----	60-130
Minolta Apo	300	2,8	----	1800-2500

Minolta Apo nero	80-200	2,8	----	710-720
Minolta Apo (D)	100-300	4,5-5,6	----	250-350
Minolta Apo G	600	4	----	5000-6100
Minolta Apo G	70-200	2,8	----	1375-1700
Minolta Apo Macro	200	4	----	1800-2150
Minolta Fisheye	16	2,8	----	400-600
Minolta G	28-70	2,8	----	610-800
Minolta G	35	1,4	----	800-1000
Minolta G	85	1,4	----	700-850
Minolta Hs Apo G	600	4	----	5500-7100
Minolta Hs-Apo G	300	4	----	1000-1300
Minolta Hs-Apo G	80-200	2,8	----	1100-1300
Minolta Hs-Apo G	200	2,8	----	950-1300
Minolta Hs-Apo G	300	2,8	----	2200-2900
Minolta Hs-Apo G	400	4,5	----	2100-2750
Minolta Macro	50	2,8	----	180-250
Minolta Macro	50	3,5	----	175-225
Minolta Original	28-85	3,5-4,5	----	59-120
Minolta Reflex	500	8	----	490-650
Minolta Shutter	35-80	4-5,6	----	29-55
Minolta Soft Focus	100	2,8	----	550-750
Minolta Stf	135	2,8	----	1000-1300

Mir

Modello	Focale	f	Attacco	€
Mir20 M Mc	20	3,5	M42	140-180
Mir 1B	37	2,8	Nikon	70-100
Mir 1	37	2,8	Kiev	40-70
Mir 10 A	28	3,5	M42	140-180
Mir 24 M Mc	35	2	M42	65-95
Mir 24 N Mc	35	2	Nikon Ai	140-160
26 B	45	3,5	Kiev 80	35-55
Mir 47 K	20	2,5	Pentax K	250-300

Miranda

Modello	Focale	f	Attacco	€
Miranda	80-200	4,5	M42	20-30
Miranda	70-210	4,5-5,6	Minolta	20-40
Miranda	135	2,8	----	70-100
Miranda Auto	50	1,4	----	40-55
Miranda Auto	135	3,5	----	28-45
Miranda Auto	50	1,8	----	48-80
Miranda Auto	135	2,8	----	28-50
Miranda Auto	35	2,8	----	45-70
Miranda Auto	105	2,8	----	45-70
Miranda Auto	200	3,5	----	65-90
Miranda Auto	50	1,9	----	32-52
Miranda Auto E	50	1,4	----	70-100
Miranda Auto Ec	28	2,8	----	110-160
Miranda Auto Ec	40	1,4	----	85-120
Miranda Macro	35-135	3,5-4,5	----	30-60
Miranda Macron	52	2,8	----	170-240
Miranda Mc Macro	75-200	4,5-5,3	Pentax K	45-72

Mitakon

Modello	Focale	f	Attacco	€
Macro	28-80	3,5-4,5	Pentax	30-50
Macro	28-200	3,8-5,5	Canon	55-80
Mc	80-200	4,5	Contax	30-50
Mc	70-210	3,5-4,5	Nikon Ais	45-70
Mc	75-240	4,5	Pentax	45-70
Mc	85-300	5,6	Olympus	25-45
Mc	35-200	3,5-4,5	Yashica	40-70
Mc	35-70	3,5-4,5	Pentax K	45-60
Mc	75-150	3,9	Yashica	28-40
Mitakon	28	2,8	Minolta	20-40
Mitakon	50	1,7	Pentax Pk	30-60

Naigon

Modello	Focale	f	Attacco	€
Naigon	28-70	3,5-4,5	Canon	80-100
Naigon	35-70	2,8-3,8	Canon	80-100
Naigon	35-70	2,8-3,8	Canon	50-90

Nicola Perscheid

Modello	Focale	f	Attacco	€
Busg A-G Rathenow	420	4,5	----	2500-3500

Nikon

Modello	Focale	f	Attacco	€
Nikkor Af	300	4	Nikon	400-600
Nikkor Af	70-210	4-5,6	----	120-150
Nikkor Af	80-400	4,5-5,6	----	750-850
Nikkor Af	24-120	3,5-5,6	----	220-280
Nikkor Af D	80-200	4,5-5,6	----	80-110
Nikkor Af G nero	70-300	4-5,6	----	90-120
Nikkor Af-S	16-85	3,5-5,6	----	380-450
Nikkor Afs Dx	18-135	3,5-5,6	Nikon	120-180
Nikkor Af-S Dx If	12-244	----	----	560-620
Nikkor Micro Af	105	2,8	Nikon	280-370
Nikon Af	80-200	2,8	Nikon	450-550
Nikon Afs	24-85	3,5	Nikon	400-500
Nikon Afs	24-120	4	Nikon	800-1000
Nikon Afs	16-85	3,5-5,6	Nikon	350-450
Nikon Afs Asp	24-120	3,5-5,6	Nikon	280-360
Nikon All nero	135	3,5	Nikon	180-220
Nikon nero	135	3,5	Nikon	100-140
Nikon Chrome	135	3,5	Nikon	80-120
Nikon El	50	2,8	Pe	45-70

Nikon Micro Nikkor Ais	200	4	Nikon	300-400
Nikon Nikkor	180	2,8	Nikon	270-320
Nikon Nikkor	20	3,5	Nikon	280-360
Nikon Nikkor	200	4	Nikon	80-120
Nikon Nikkor	21	4	Nikon	550-650
Nikon Nikkor	50-300	4,5	Nikon	270-320
Nikon Nikkor Af	105	2	Nikon	850-950
Nikon Nikkor Af	105	2	Nikon	700-820
Nikon Nikkor Af	135	2	Nikon	850-950
Nikon Nikkor Af	200	2	Nikon	4000-5000
Nikon Nikkor Af	20-35	2,8	Nikon	500-600
Nikon Nikkor Af	200	2	Nikon	4000-5000
Nikon Nikkor Af	20-35	2,8	Nikon	500-600
Nikon Nikkor Af Aspherical	14	2,8	Nikon	700-820
Nikon Nikkor Af	14	2,8	Nikon	720-820
Nikon Nikkor Af Aspherical	24-120	4	Nikon	800-900
Nikon Nikkor Afs Aspherical	14-24	2,8	Nikon	900-1200
Nikon Nikkor Afs Aspherical	18-35	3,5-4,5	Nikon	280-380
Nikon Nikkor Ai	43-86	3,5	Nikon	60-90
Nikon Nikkor Ai	50	1,4	Nikon	100-140
Nikon Nikkor Ai	55	3,5	Nikon	100-140
Nikon Nikkor Ai	80-200	4,5	Nikon	60-90
Nikon Nikkor Ai	80-200	4,5	Nikon	80-100
Nikon Nikkor Ai	135	3,5	----	80-100
Nikon Nikkor Ais	35-105	3,5-4,5	Nikon	70-90
Nikon Nikkor Ais	35-135	3,5-4,5	Nikon	180-200
Nikon Nikkor M	200	8	----	520-700
Nikon Nikkor M	300	9	----	620-780
Nikon Nikkor M	450	9	----	2300-2500

Nikon Nikkor Micro	55	3,5	Nikon	120-170
Nikon Nikkor Reflex	500	8	Nikon	250-290
Nikon Nikkor Sw	65	4	----	950-1100
Nikon Nikkor Sw	75	4,5	----	1100-1300
Nikon Nikkor Sw	90	8	----	750-900
Nikon Nikkor Sw	90	4,5	----	1200-1400
Nikon Nikkor Sw	120	8	----	1000-1200
Nikon Nikkor Sw	150	8	----	2200-2350
Nikon Nikkor T Ed	270	6,3	----	1350-1550
Nikon Nikkor T Ed	360	8	----	1850-2000
Nikon Nikkor T Ed	500	11	----	1850-2000
Nikon Nikkor T Ed	600	9	----	2600-2700
Nikon Nikkor T Ed	720	16	----	1900-2200
Nikon Nikkor T Ed	800	12	----	2800-3000
Nikon Nikkor T Ed	1200	18	----	2200-2350
Nikon Nikkor W	105	5,6	----	400-590
Nikon Nikkor W	135	5,6	----	500-690
Nikon Nikkor W	150	5,6	----	460-650
Nikon Nikkor W	180	5,6	----	560-750
Nikon Nikkor W	210	5,6	----	580-750
Nikon Nikkor W	240	5,6	----	1100-1250
Nikon Nikkor W	300	5,6	----	1450-1600
Nikon Nikkor W	360	6,5	----	1500-1700

Nikula

Modello	Focale	f	Attacco	€
Nikula 8x60s	800	8	Sony Alpha	180-250
Nikula 8x60s	800	8	Nikon	180-250
Nikula 8x60s	800	8	Canon	180-250
Nikula 8x60s	800	8	Pentax	160-240
Nikula 8x60s	800	8	Olympus 4/3	170-240
Nikula 8x60s	800	8	Micro 4/3	160-220

Novoflex

Modello	Focale	f	Attacco	€
Auto	105	3,5	----	160-190
Auto	105	4	Contax	220-260
Noflexar Mf	400	5,6	----	150-250
Noflexar Mf	600	8	----	150-250
Noflexar Mf	300	5,6	Exakta	280-350

Norisstar

Modello	Focale	f	Attacco	€
Norisstar	150	3,5	----	50-80
Norisstar	150	3,5	Projector	20-45

Ocean

Modello	Focale	f	Attacco	€
Ocean	75	3,5	----	18-40
Ocean	135	3,5	M42	55-80
Ocean	28	2,8	----	50-70

Officine Galileo

Modello	Focale	f	Attacco	€
Aerostigmat	300	4,5	----	120-160
Inora	50	3,5	----	28-45
Neocinar	160	----	Projector	140-190
Neocinar	180	----	Projector	150-200
Ogmar	90	4	L39	600-800
Repho	50	3,5	----	35-55

Olympus

Modello	Focale	f	Attacco	€
Af	70-210	3,5-4,5	----	25-40
Lh-70 Zuiko	14-54	2,8-3,5	----	35-55
Lh-70b Zuiko	50-200	2,8-3,5	----	35-55
M.Zuiko Digital	75	1,8	----	400-500
Om	35-70	----	Olympus	100-150
Om	40	2	Canon	250-300
Olympus	80-200	----	----	35-55
Om Zuiko	75-150	4	----	70-120
Om Zuiko	85-250	5	----	150-250
Om Zuiko Macro	50	3,5	----	100-150
Om Zuiko Mc	28	2	----	180-350
Power Focus Af	35-70	3,5-4,5	----	20-35
Zuiko	13	3,5	----	28-45
Zuiko	28	3,5	----	20-35
Zuiko	135	3,5	----	55-80
Zuiko	35-70	4	----	45-70
Zuiko	50	1,8	----	35-50
Zuiko	60	2,8	Micro 4/3	180-220
Zuiko	14-42	3,5-5,6	----	55-80
Zuiko	75-150	4	----	25-45
Zuiko Af Ed Pro	12-40	2,8	----	450-550
Zuiko Auto-S	50	1,8	Om	25-50
Zuiko Digital	70-300	4-5,6	4/3	140-180
Zuiko Digital	25	1,8	----	160-200
Zuiko Digital	40-150	3,5-4,5	----	35-55
Zuiko Digital Ed	8	1,8	----	500-600
Zuiko Digital Ed	40-150	2,8	----	650-750
Zuik Ed argento	40-150	4,0-5,6	----	80-110
Zuiko Om	65-200	4	----	150-200
Zuiko Om	100	2,8	----	90-120
Zuiko Om AutoT	85	2	----	160-200
Super Ozeck Macro	75-150	3,8	----	28-40

Optomax

Modello	Focale	f	Attacco	€
Optomax	135	3,5	M42	30-50
Optomax	28	2,8	Olympus	70-90
Optomax	35	2,8	M42	40-70
Optomax	135	2,8	M42	40-70
Optomax	300	5,6	M42	75-100
Optomax	200	4,5	M42	45-70
Optomax	85-205	3,5	M42	40-70

Osawa

Modello	Focale	f	Attacco	€
Osawa Mc Mf	28	2,8	Canon Fd	30-55
Osawa	80-205	4,5	----	29-45
Osawa	70-140	3,8	----	25-50
Osawa Macro	28-80	3,-4,5	Mamiya	28-45
Osawa Mc	38-70	3,5	----	25-45
Osawa Mc	75-150	3,8	----	24-40
Osawa Mc	135	2,8	Mamiya	25-50
Osawa Mc Macro	80-205	4,5	Contax	28-45
Osawa Mf	28-50	3,5-4,5	----	32-47
Osawa Mf	650	8,5	Nikon	30-60
Tominon El	75	4,5	----	40-60

Panagor

Modello	Focale	f	Attacco	€
Panagor	135	2,8	Konica	20-40
Panagor	28	2,8	Minolta	35-55
Panagor	80-200	3,8	Minolta	29-42
Panagor	35-100	3,5	Canon	80-120
Panagor	80-200	3,9	Canon	45-85
Panagor Mc	28	2,8	Pentax Ka	30-45

Panasonic

Modello	Focale	f	Attacco	€
Lumix Pancake	14	2,5	----	200-240
Panasonic	14-42	3,5-5,6	----	250-290
Panasonic	45-150	4-5,6	----	280-320
Panasonic	42,5	1,7	----	280-350
Panasonic	8	3,5	----	550-650
Panasonic	45-175	4-5,6	----	350-380
Panasonic Asp	20	1,7	----	140-180
Panasonic G	12,5	1,2	----	190-240
Panasonic G Asp	20	1,7	4/3	240-290
Panasonic G Asp	42,5	1,2	----	800-1000
Panasonic G Vario	12-32	3,5-5,6	----	280-310
Panasonic G Vario	7-14	4	----	550-650
Panasonic G Vario	14-40	3,5-5,6	----	350-470
Panasonic G Vario	100-300	4-5,6	----	350-450
Panasonic G Vario	45-200	4-5,6	----	240-280
Panasonic G Vario	35-100	4-5,6	----	350-400
Panasonic G Vario	12-35	2,8	----	280-320
Panasonic G X Vario	35-100	2,8	----	800-950

Peleng

Modello	Focale	f	Attacco	€
Belomo	17	2,8	M42	200-250
Fisheye	8	3,5	Micro 4/3	270-320
Fisheye	8	3,5	Sony NEX	260-300
Fisheye	8	3,5	Minolta Md	270-320
Fisheye	8	3,5	Canon FD	270-320
Fisheye	8	3,5	Samsung NX	270-320
Fisheye	8	3,5	Contax/Yashica	270-320
Fisheye	8	3,5	Nikon	260-300

Pentacon

Modello	Focale	f	Attacco	€
Pentacon	135	2,8	M42	140-180
Pentacon	200	4	M42	140-160
Pentacon	30	3,5	M42	95-140
Pentacon Auto	50	1,8	M42	60-90
Pentacon Auto	100	2,8	M42	160-190
Pentacon Electric	29	2,8	M42	145-200
Pentacon Mc	29	2,8	M42	28-50
Pentacon Prakticar	50	2,4	----	28-45

Pentax

Modello	Focale	f	Attacco	€
Asahi Pentax	50	1,4	----	80-100
Asahi Pentax	150	4	----	120-160
Asahi Pentax Macro	135	4	6x7	190-250
Asahi Pentax A	16	2,8	K	350-450
Pentax	28-80	3,5-5,6	K	35-55
Pentax	50	1,7	K	45-70
Pentax	70	2,80	----	80-100
Pentax	45	4	6x7	85-120
Pentax	300	6,3	M42	70-95
Pentax	55	4	6x7	40-60
Pentax	50	2	----	40-60
Pentax	50	1,4	Vite	80-120
Pentax	50	1,2	----	400-480
Pentax	50	1,4	Vite	80-120
Pentax	50	1,2	----	400-480
Pentax	55	2,2	M42	70-110
Pentax	28-50	3,5-4,5	----	120-145

Pentax	18-55	3-5,6	----	50-75
Pentax	35	2,4	----	80-120
Pentax 645	75	2,8	----	190-250
Pentax 645	150	3,5	----	180-260
Pentax 645	55	2,8	----	180-220
Pentax 67	165	2,8	----	150-210
Pentax 67	300	4	----	350-450
Pentax 67	200	4	----	150-200
Pentax 67	300	4	----	180-240
Pentax 67 Macro	100	4	----	350-450
Pentax Af	35-80	4-5,6	----	40-60
Pentax Af	28-70	4	----	50-80
Pentax Da	35	2,4	----	75-110
Pentax Ed Limited	15	4	----	450-550
Pentax Fa	55-110	5,6	----	450-550
Pentax Fa	45-85	4,5	----	450-550
Pentax Fa	43	1,9	----	350-450
Pentax M	40	2,8	----	35-55
Pentax Macro	40-80	2,8-4	----	50-75
Pentax Macro	28-80	3,5-4,5	----	120-140
Pentax Mf	28	2,8	----	25-40
Pentax Prime	8,5	1,9	----	120-160
Pentax Q	3.2	5,6	----	70-100
Pentax Smc	55-300	4-5,8	----	80-120
Pentax Smc	120	2,8	----	170-220
Pentax Smc	21	3,2	Da	250-290
Pentax Smc	135	3,5	----	60-90
Pentax Smc	50-200	4-5,6	----	100-125
Pentax Smc	135	3,5	----	45-60
Pentax Smc (1975)	55	1,8	----	15-25
Pentax Smc Af	80-200	4,7-5,6	----	50-80
Pentax Smc Macro	70-210	4	----	120-160

Petzval

Modello	Focale	f	Attacco	€
Petzval	225	4	----	600-800
Petzval	200	6,6	----	200-400
Petzval	300	8	----	400-550
Petzval	210	3,5	Graflex	300-450
Petzval fatto di ottone	85	2,2	----	500-700
Petzval fatto di ottone	440	----	----	200-400
Petzval fatto di ottone	100	4,5	----	200-400
Petzval fatto di ottone per collodio	----	----	----	300-450
Petzval fatto di ottone per dagherrotipi	----	----	----	400-600

Phokinar

Modello	Focale	f	Attacco	€
Phokinar	135	2,8	M42	60-80
Phokinar	200	3,5	M42	35-60

Porst

Modello	Focale	f	Attacco	€
Color Reflex	55	1,4	M42	55-90
Color Reflex Auto	55	2,8	M42	25-40
Color Reflex D	50	1,9	----	20-40
Color Reflex Mc	55	1,2	Nikon	150-190
Color Reflex Mc Auto	50	1,4	----	35-55
Color Reflex Mc Auto	55	1,4	M42	40-55
Color Reflex Mc Auto	50	1,7	M42	50-80
Color Reflex Umc	50	1,6	----	30-50
Mc	50	1,4	Sony	60-90
Porst	28	2,8	Fujica	30-50
Porst	50	1,9	Fujica	40-60

Porst	135	2,8	Pentax K	29-45
Porst	35	2,8	M42	28-45
Porst Super-Ww	28	2,8	M42	28-40
Tele	135	3,5	M42	30-50
Tele Auto D	200	3,3	M42	70-95
Tele Gmc	135	2,8	----	30-50
Tele Mc Auto D	135	2,8	Pentax K	40-60
Tele-Zoom-As Mc/Macro	75-200	3,8	Pentax K	40-70
Uni-Zoom Macro	35-105	3,5	Pentax K	40-70
Ww Macro	24	3,5	----	55-90
Ww-Macro	28	2,8	----	60-85

Polaroid

Modello	Focale	f	Attacco	€
Polaroid (shutter)	17	4	----	90-125
Studio Series	52	2,2	----	25-45
Studio Series Macro.X43	58	----	----	20-50
Super telephoto 42X	----	----	-----	40-70
Tominon (shutter)	135	4,5	----	50-85
Tominon (shutter)	75	4	----	80-120

Prinzflex

Modello	Focale	f	Attacco	€
Auto	100-200	5,6	M42	20-40
Auto Reflex	135	3,5	----	25-40
Auto Reflex	135	2,8	M42	20-40
Auto Reflex	200	3,5	M42	20-40
Mc	70-162	----	Pentax Pk	20-40
Mc Zoom	35-70	3,5-4,5	Pentax K	20-40

Prinzflex	80-200	4,5-5,6	M42	20-30
Prinzflex	100	2,8	M42	25-45
Prinzflex	28	2,8	M42	20-40
Prinzflex	23	3,5	M42	35-55
Prinzflex	200	3,3	Pentax K	35-50
Prinzflex	35	5,6	Pentax-K	40-60
Prinzflex	135	2,8	Pentax K	22-42
Super Ttl	55	1,7	----	22-40

Revuenon

Modello	Focale	f	Attacco	€
Revuenon	135	2,8	Vite M42	60-80
Revuenon	240	4	----	45-65
Revuenon	55	1,2	Pentax Pk	350-400
Revuenon	85-205	3,9	M42	120-180
Revuenon Auto	55	2,8	M42	40-60
Revuenon Auto	55	2	M42	25-40
Revuenon Auto	55	1,4	M42	120-150
Revuenon Auto	35-100	3,5-4	Pk	45-60
Revuenon Auto	55	1,4	M42	85-120
Revuenon Auto Mc	50	1,4	Pentax K	70-95
Revuenon Auto Mc	80-200	4,5	----	120-180
Revuenon Mc Macro	24	4	M42	120-150
Revuenon Mc Macro	28	3,5	M42	90-120
Revuenon Special Mf	35	2,8	M42	30-50
Revuenon Ultra	55	4	----	25-45

Rodenstock

Modello	Focale	f	Attacco	€
Apo-Grandagon N	35	4,5	----	1000-1200
Apo-Grandagon N	45	4,5	----	800-1000
Apo-Grandagon N	55	4,5	----	1000-1200
Apo-Ronar	150	9	----	550-750
Apo-Ronar	240	9	----	1000-1200
Apo-Ronar	300	9	----	1100-1300
Apo-Ronar	360	9	----	1350-1550
Apo-Ronar	480	9	----	2100-2300
Apo-Sironar N	100	5,6	----	399-599
Apo-Sironar N	135	5,6	----	400-600
Apo-Sironar N	150	5,6	----	450-650
Apo-Sironar N	180	5,6	----	650-850
Apo-Sironar N	210	5,6	----	600-800
Apo-Sironar N	240	5,6	----	1200-1400
Apo-Sironar N	300	5,6	----	1700-1900
Apo-Sironar N	360	6,8	----	1850-2050
Apo-Sironar N	480	8,4	----	3000-3200
Apo-Sironar S	135	5,6	----	500-700
Apo-Sironar S	150	5,6	----	550-750
Apo-Sironar S	180	5,6	----	700-900
Apo-Sironar S	210	5,6	----	850-1050
Apo-Sironar S	240	5,6	----	1560-1760
Apo-Sironar S	300	5,6	----	1900-2100
Apo-Sironar S	360	6,8	----	2390-2590
Apo-Sironar W	150	5,6	----	1000-1200
Apo-Sironar W	210	5,6	----	1699-1899
Apo-Sironar W	300	5,6	----	2800-3000
Grandagon N	65	4,5	----	1100-1300
Grandagon N	75	4,5	----	1000-1200
Grandagon N	75	6,8	----	649-849
Grandagon N	90	4,5	----	1200-1400
Grandagon N	90	6,8	----	819-1019
Grandagon N	115	6,8	----	1300-1500

Grandagon N	155	6,8	----	2800-3000
Grandagon N	200	6,8	----	4400-4600
Omegaron	50	3,5	Pe	55-70
Omegaron	90	4,5	Pe	60-80
Rodagon	60	5,6	----	70-100
Rodagon	50	4,5	----	80-120
Rodagon	50	2,8	----	250-300
Rodagon	135	5,6	----	170-220
Rodagon	105	5,6	----	140-200
Rodagon	150	5,6	Pe	80-120
Rodagon	50	5,6	Pe	60-95
Rodenstock	150	5,6	----	80-120
Rodenstock	210	5,6	----	70-90
Rogonar	50	2,8	Pe	60-90
Sironar	150	5,6	----	380-480
Sironar-N	360	6,8	----	600-800
Sironar-N	240	5,6	----	400-550

Roeschlein Kreuznach

Modello	Focale	f	Attacco	€
Angluon	90	6,8	Lf	80-140
Componar	50	2,8	Pe	18-28
Componar	75	4 5	----	45-85
Componon	80	5,6	----	20-50
Curtagon	35	4	Pentax Pk	180-240
E Telenar	90	3,8	M39	80-110
Radiogon	35	4	----	70-100
Retina-Curtagon	28	4	----	45-75
Super Angulon	90	2,8	----	170-210
Stellar	55	2,8	Projector	18-30
Super Angulon Mc	90	8	----	140-180
Symmar	150	5,6	----	60-90

Symmar	210	5,6	----	70-95
Symmar	150	5,6	----	80-110
Symmar	300	5,6	----	290-350
Tele-Arton	270	5,5	----	120-160
Telenar	135	5,6	M39	80-120
Tele-Xenar	135	4	----	50-80
Variogon	18-90	2	Micro 4/3	400-550
Variogon Macro	140-280	5,6	Hasselblad V	800-950
Xenar	210	4,5	----	110-140
Xenar	50	2,8	M42	70-90
Xenar	38	2,8	----	35-60
Xenoplan	50	2,8	C-Mount	140-180

Rollei

Modello	Focale	f	Attacco	€
Rollei Heidosmat	90	2,4	Projector	50-80
Rollei Hft Distagon	50	4	----	280-360
Rollei Hft Sonnar	250	5,6	----	250-350
Rollei Planar	50	1,4	----	150-200
Rollei Planar macro	120	5,6	----	550-640
Rollei Planar Sl	50	1,8	----	120-160
Rollei Rolleigon	150	4	----	280-350
Rollei Rolleinar	80-200	4	----	160-220
Rollei Rolleinar	28	2,8	----	120-150
Rollei Rolleinar Mc	35-105	3,5	----	120-160
Rollei Rolleinar Mc	21	4	----	250-350
Rollei Rolleinar Mc	200	3,5	----	250-350
Rollei Rolleinar Mc	200	3,5	----	90-140
Rollei Sonnar	150	4	----	550-650
Rollei Heidosmat	110-160	3,5	Projector	80-120
Rolleiflex Planar	80	2,8	----	400-500
Rolleinar-Mc	135	2.8	Rollei	80-100
Rollri Rolleinar Apo	70-210	3,5-4,5	----	350-440

Samyang

Modello	Focale	f	Attacco	€
Samyang	8	3,5	Olympus	250-350
Samyang	12	2	Sony	250-350
Samyang	10	2,8	Canon Eos	280-360
Samyang	650-1300	8-16	4/3	180-220
Samyang	500	8	----	85-100
Samyang	85	1,4	Canon	250-350
Samyang	7,5	3,5	Micro 4/3	200-250
Samyang	14	2,8	----	250-290
Samyang	12	2	Sony E	100-140
Samyang	24	3,5	Sony E	500-700
Samyang	16	2	Fuji-X	200-250
Samyang	35	1,4	Canon Ef	370-420
Samyang	500	8	Canon	140-180
Samyang	300	6,3	4/3	280-320
Samyang	12	2,8	Pentax	420-480
Samyang As Umc	35	1,4	Sony	190-250
Samyang Asfmc	8	3,5	----	180-220
Samyang Catad.	800	8	----	180-220
Samyang Fisheye	8	3,5	Canon Eos	200-300
Samyang Mc	500	6,3	Canon	170-220
Samyang Umc	43	1,4	4/3	450-550
Samyang Umc	8	2,8	----	180-260
Samyang Umc	7.5	3,5	Micro 4/3	180-250
Samyang Umc	24	1,4	Olympus	360-450
Samyang Umc	135	2	Pentax	480-520
Samyangasf	85	1,4	Nikon	140-170
Samyangumc	8	3,8	Olympus	320-380

Schast

Modello	Focale	f	Attacco	€
Schacht Travegon	35	3,5	Exakta	45-70
Travenar	135	3,5	Exacta	75-100

Schneider

Modello	Focale	f	Attacco	€
Angulon	90	8	Sinar	450-550
Apo-Symmar	100	5,6	----	400-600
Apo-Symmar	120	5,6	----	500-700
Apo-Symmar	135	5,6	----	500-700
Apo-Symmar	150	5,6	----	500-700
Apo-Symmar	180	5,6	----	700-900
Apo-Symmar	210	5,6	----	700-900
Apo-Symmar	240	5,6	----	1100-1300
Apo-Symmar	300	5,6	----	1600-1800
Apo-Symmar	360	6,8	----	1800-2000
Apo-Symmar	480	8,4	----	2300-2500
Apo-Tele Xenar HM	800	12	----	8700-8900
Apo-Tele-Xenar HM	400	5,6	----	300-500
Apo-Tele-Xenar HM Compact	400	5,6	----	2100-2300
Componar	75	4,5	Pe	60-85
Componon	210	5,6	Pe	90-140
Componon	28	4	Pe	90-140
G-Claron	150	9	----	400-600
G-Claron	210	9	----	600-800
G-Claron	240	9	----	600-800
G-Claron	270	9	----	800-1000
G-Claron	305	9	----	800-1000
G-Claron	355	9	----	1300-1500
Schneider	360	5,5	----	400-500
Super Angulon	121	8	----	400-500
Super-Angulon	47	5,6	----	800-1000
Super-Angulon	65	5,6	----	1000-1200
Super-Angulon	75	5,6	----	1100-1300
Super-Angulon	90	5,6	----	1300-1500
Super-Angulon	90	8	----	800-1000
Super-Angulon	120	8	----	1200-1400

Super-Angulon	165	8	----	3100-3300
Super-Angulon	210	8	----	5000-5200
Super-Angulon XL	38	5,6	----	1200-1400
Super-Angulon XL	47	5,6	----	1200-1400
Super-Angulon XL	58	5,6	----	1000-1200
Super-Angulon XL	72	5,6	----	1300-1500
Super-Angulon XL	90	5,6	----	1400-1600
Super-Symmar HM	120	5,6	----	1100-1300
Super-Symmar HM	150	5,6	----	1500-1700
Super-Symmar HM	210	5,6	----	2500-2700
Super-Symmar XL	80	4,5	----	1400-1600
Super-Symmar XL	110	5,6	----	1500-1700
Super-Symmar XL	150	5,6	----	2000-2200
Super-Symmar XL	210	5,6	----	2700-2900
Symmar	240	5,6	----	450-550
Symmar Apo	240	5,6	----	800-1000
Tele-Arton	250	5,6	----	140-200
Xenar	180	4,5	----	70-90
Xenar	150	5,6	----	200-400
Xenar	210	6,1	----	500-700

Schneider -Kreusnach

Modello	Focale	f	Attacco	€
Super Angulon	40	3,5	Rollei	1200-1500
Super Angulon	65	8	----	350-400
Super Angulon	90	8	----	250-300
Symmar otturatore	240	5,6	----	180-250
Tele exanar	180	2,8	Rollei	1200-1400

Schulze & Billerbeck

Modello	Focale	f	Attacco	€
Goerlitz Euryplan Series II (brass)	300	6,5	----	220-290

Seimar

Modello	Focale	f	Attacco	€
Donnex	80-200	4,5	Olympus Om	50-70
Donnex	80-200	4,5	Fuji X	28-45
Donnex	28- 80	3,9-4,9	Olympus Om	30-50
Macro	60-300	4-5,6	Sony Minolta	140-170
Seimar	35-70	3,5-4,5	Canon	70-90
Seimar	35-70	3,5-4,5	Canon	50-80
Seimar	28	2,8	Nikon Ai	60-80
Seimar	70-210	4,5	Minolta Md	55-75
Seimar	200	4	T2	20-40
Seimar Auto Mc	28	2,8	M42	20-40
Seimar Macro	28-200	3,5-5,5	Canon Ae-1	170-210
Seimar Macro	28-70	3,9-4,8	Canon Ae-1	95-125
Seimar Mc Macro	28-70	3,9-4,8	Contax	90-120
Seimar Mc Macro	28-70	3,9-4,8	Canon Fd	60-80
Seimar Mc Zoom Macro	24-70	3,5-4,8	Nikon Ai	95-120
Seimar Mc Zoom Macro	24-70	3,5-4,8	Olympus Om	80-100

Sesnon

Modello	Focale	f	Attacco	€
Sesnon	35	2,8	----	30-50
Sesnon Auto	135	2,8	M42	20-40
Sesnon Auto	70-215	3,8	----	30-45

Sigma

Modello	Focale	f	Attacco	€
Sigma	10-20	4-5,6	Canon Eos	250-320
Sigma	21-35	3,5-4,2	----	70-90
Sigma	18-200	3,5-6,3	----	150-250
Sigma	21-35	3,5-4,2	Pentax K	80-140
Sigma	28-105	2,8-4	Pentax K	120-140
Sigma	150-600	----	Canon	1000-2000
Sigma	70-210	4-5,6	Olympus Om	40-60
Sigma	24	2,8	Canon Fd	70-90
Sigma	135	3,5	Canon	40-80
Sigma	28-70	2,8	Canon	140-170
Sigma	70-150	3,5	Canon	45-65
Sigma	135	3,5	Canon	45-80
Sigma	28-70	3,5-4,5	Yashica	40-60
Sigma	28-200	3,8-5,6	----	100-140
Sigma	21-35	3,5-4,2	----	100-140
Sigma	18-35	3,5-4,5	----	170-200
Sigma	80-200	4,5-5,6	M42	25-35
Sigma Af	28-105	2,8-4	Pentax K	110-150
Sigma Af	18-50	2,8	Nikon	200-250
Sigma Af	24-70	2,8	----	400-450
Sigma Af	100-300	4,5-6,7	Pentax	50-75
Sigma Af	75-300	4,5-5,6	----	65-90

Sigma Af Macro Asp	28-135	3,8-5,6	----	70-95
Sigma Apo	135-400	4,5-5,6	Canon	160-190
Sigma Apo	70-210	3,5-4-5	Minolta	50-75
Sigma Apo Dg	70-300	4-5,6	Canon	90-150
Sigma Apo Dg Af	100-300	4	Nikon	380-450
Sigma Apo Dg Os	120-400	4,5-5,6	Nikon	350-450
Sigma Apo Macro	150	2,8	Canon Eos	350-450
Sigma D	18-35	3,5-4,5	Nikon	120-140
Sigma D	28-300	3,5-6,3	----	140-160
Sigma Dc	55-200	4-5,6	----	40-60
Sigma Dg Os	70-300	4-5,6	Canon	160-220
Sigma Ex	28-70	2,8	----	150-200
Sigma Ex Asp	14	2,8	Pentax	220-280
Sigma Ex Dc	10-20	4-5,6	----	300-400
Sigma Ex Dc Macro	18-50	2,8	----	300-400
Sigma Ex Dg Hsm	50	1,4	Canon Eos	280-360
Sigma Hsm Dc	8-16	4,5-5,6	----	500-600
Sigma Macro Dg	50	2,8	----	220-260
Sigma Macro Dc	18-50	2,8	----	270-320
Sigma Mc Mini-Wide	28	2,8	Pentax	40-55
Sigma Mini Wide	28	2,8	Olympus	35-55
Sigma Super Wide	24	2,8	Canon	40-60
Sigma Uc	70-210	4-5,6	Pentax-A	50-80

Sinar

Modello	Focale	f	Attacco	€
Sinar Apo	305	9	----	200-250
Sinaron	300	5,6	----	280-350
Sinaron	360	6,8	----	350-400
Sinaron	180	5,6	----	185-210
Sinaron (shutter)	150	5,6	----	180-250
Sinaron (shutter)	90	8	----	1800-2000
Sinaron Digital	80	4	----	400-500
Sinaron Digital	105	4	----	350-450
Sinaron Digital	80	2,8	----	280-320
Sinaron Digital Af	80	2,8	----	500-600
Sinaron Digital Macro	120	5,6	----	800-1000
Sinaron Mc	210	5,6	----	490-550
Sinaron Mc	65	4,5	----	480-520
Sinaron Mc	240	5,6	----	280-350
Sironar Db-M	240	5,6	----	500-800

Sirius

Modello	Focale	f	Attacco	€
Sirius	80-200	3,9	M42	25-45
Sirius	28-70	3,5-4,5	----	28-50
Sirius	60-300	4-5,6	M42	30-50
Sirius	28-200	4-5,6	Praktica	40-65
Sirius Macro Mc	500	8	----	60-90
Sirius Mc	135	2,8	M42	40-60
Sirius Mc Auto	18-28	----	Minolta Xg	30-50
Sirius Mc Auto	28-85	3,5-4,5	Pentax	18-35
Sirius Mc Auto	35-135	3,5-4,5	Fujica Fx	28-45
Sirius Mc Automatic	28	2,8	Pentax	28-50

Società Anonima Ambrosio

Modello	Focale	f	Attacco	€
Cine	----	----	----	160-280

Soligor

Modello	Focale	f	Attacco	€
Soligor	80-200	4,5	----	65-85
Soligor	28	2,8	Pentax K	28-45
Soligor	28	2,8	Olympus	25-45
Soligor	50	1,9	Miranda	45-70
Soligor	28	2,5	Nikon Ai	35-50
Soligor	28	2,8	Nikon Ai	35-55
Soligor	135	3,5	M42	28-45
Soligor	135	2,8	Exakta	28-45
Soligor	35	3,5	M42	30-50
Soligor	100-300	5	----	20-40
Soligor	105	2,8	Exacta	35-60
Soligor	28-200	3,8-5,5	Pentax	29-45
Soligor	200	4,5	----	28-55
Soligor	500	8	Canon	50-80
Soligor	24-45	3,5-4,5	Canon Fd	50-80
Soligor	350	5,6	Pk	45-70
Soligor	250	4,5	M42	28-45
Soligor Af	19-35	3,5-4,5	Pentax	80-100
Soligor Af	28-80	3,5-5,6	----	40-55
Soligor Auto	35	2,8	M42	30-50
Soligor Macro	60-300	4-5,6	----	65-85
Soligor Macro	85-205	3,8	----	25-45
Soligor Macro	28-80	3,5-4,5	Pentax	25-45
Soligor Macro	35-80	3,5-4,8	Pentax K	25-45
Soligor Mc	135	2,5	Olympus	35-55
Soligor Mc Macro	35-70	2,5-3,5	Contax	30-60
Soligor Md	28	2,8	Minolta	25-45
Soligor Mf /Md	28-105	3,5-4,5	Minolta	70-100
Soligor Tele-Auto	200	3,5	M42	30-50

Som Berthiot

Modello	Focale	f	Attacco	€
Cinor	10	1,9	C	65-95
Cinor	50	1,5	----	70-100
Cinor	25	1,8	C	70-110
Cinor	25	1,9	C	50-85
Cinor	23	2,3	D	40-65
Cinor	20	1,5	----	170-210
Cinor	35	3,5	D	100-120
Cinor	25	0,95	C	600-700
Eidoscope 2	375	4,5	----	1000-1200
Lytar	16	2,8	C	120-160
Pan Cinor	37-150	5	----	80-120
Pan Cinor	17,5-70	2,4	C	300-400
Pan-Cinor	10-30	2,8	----	60-90
Pan-Cinor	25-100	----	Arriflex	650-750
Pan-Cinor	17-68	2	----	90-140
Pan-Cinor	17-85	2	C	180-250
Pan-Cinor	25-100	3,4	----	250-300
Paris	50	----	Projector	60-95
Paris	80-125	----	Projector	40-65
Paris Cinor	25	1,5	C	95-150
Paris Cinor	17	1,5	C	95-140
Paris Cinor	12.5	1,8	D	95-120
Paris Cinor	20	1,5	C	95-140
Paris Flor	50	3,5	----	180-240
Paris Olor	260	5,7	----	70-95
Paris Pan-Cinor	38-155	3,8	----	550-650
Paris Pan-Cinor	17-85	2	C	120-145
Som Berthiot	9.5-45	1,9	----	60-95
Som Berthiot	25	1,8	C	110-150

Sony

Modello	Focale	f	Attacco	€
Ae	28-70	3,5 - 5,6	----	450-500
Ae	70-200	4	----	1250-1500
Af	16	2,8	----	900-1000
Af	20	2,8	----	600-680
Af	75-300	4,5 - 5,6	----	250-300
Af	50	1,4	----	350-410
Af Dt Sam	55-300	4,5 - 5,6	----	280-350
Af G	35	1,4	----	1500-1600
Af G	70 - 200	2,8	----	1800-2200
Af G	300	2,8	----	6500-7800
Af G	500	4	----	12000-13600
Af G Ssm	70-300	4,5-5,6	----	900-1100
Af Macro 1:1	50	2,8	----	450-550
Af Macro 1:1	100	2,8	----	800-900
Af Sam	35	1,8	----	180-200
Af Sam	28 - 75	2,8	----	750-800
Af Sam	85	2,8	----	240-270
Af Stf	135	2,8	----	1200-1350
Dt Af	16 - 105	3,5-5,6	----	650-720
Dt Af	18 - 250	3,5-6,3	----	650-720
Dt Af	55 - 200	4-5,6	----	280-300
Dt Af	11 - 18	4,5-5,6	----	650-750
Dt Af Sam	18-55	3,5-5,6	----	180-220
Dt Af Sam	18 - 135	3,5-5,6	----	470-520
Dt Af Sam	50	1,8	----	140-170
Dt Ssm	16 - 50	2,8	----	640-760
G Ssm Ii	70 - 200	2,8	----	2700-3000
G Ssm Ii	70 - 400	4-5,6	----	1800-2200
Macro Dt Af	30	2,8	----	180-220
Macro Nex Af	30	3,5	----	250-280
Nex Af	16	2,8	----	220-270
Nex Af Oss	35	1,8	----	400-450
Nex Af Oss	18 - 55	3,5-5,6	----	280-320

Nex Af Oss	18 - 200	3,5-6,3	----	740-800
Nex Af Oss	55 - 210	4,5-6,3	----	280-370
Nex Af Oss	50	1,8	----	240-320
Nex Af Oss	10 - 18	4	----	750-850
Nex Af Oss	16 - 50	3,5-5,6	----	250-350
Nex Zeiss Af	24	1,8	----	950-1100
Oss	20	2,8	----	300-350
Oss	16 - 70	4	----	900-1000
Oss	18 - 200	3,5-6,3	----	760-850
Oss G	18 - 105	4	----	550-600
Sony	24-105	3,5-4,5	----	250-370
Sony	75-300	4,5-5,6	----	95-180
Sony	50	1,4	----	225-350
Sony	28	2,8	----	140-225
Sony	20	2,8	----	445-525
Sony	28	2	----	400-450
Sony	24 - 240	3,5 - 6,3	----	870-1000
Sony	28 - 135	4	----	1900-2500
Sony	90	2,8	----	950-1150
Sony G Ssm	70-300	4,5-5,6	----	700-850
Sony Cz	16-35	2,8	----	1300-1550
Sony Cz	24-70	2,8	----	1200-1700
Sony Cz	135	1,8	----	1350-1550
Sony Cz	85	1,4	----	1250-1450
Sony Cz	24	2	----	1099-1300
Sony Cz Dt	16-80	3,5-4,5	----	550-750
Sony Dt	11-18	4,5-5,6	----	480-520
Sony Dt	18-70	3,5-5,6	----	50-80
Sony Dt	18-200	3,5-6,3	----	180-250
Sony Dt	16-105	3,5-5,6	----	340-475
Sony Dt	55-200	4,0-5,6	----	85-140
Sony Dt Sam	35	1,8	----	130-175
Sony Dt Sam	18-55	3,5-5,6	----	60-90
Sony Dt Sam	55-200	4,0-5,6	----	85-150
Sony Dt 3.5-	18-250	6,3	----	350-425

Sony Dt Sam	50	1,8	----	110-150
Sony Dt Ssm	16-50	2,8	----	650-750
Sony E	35	2,8	Konica	80-120
Sony Fisheye	16	2,8	----	550-710
Sony G	70-400	4-5,6	----	1550-1750
Sony G	70-200	2,8	----	1300-1750
Sony G	300	2,8	----	4500-5500
Sony G	35	1,4	----	900-1100
Sony Macro	50	2,8	----	340-400
Sony Macro	100	2,8	----	450-600
Sony Reflex	500	8	----	550-650
Sony Sam	85	2,8	----	190-250
Sony Sam	28-75	2,8	----	475-550
Sony Stf	135	2,8	----	1120-1300
Sony Dt Macro	30	2,8	----	150-200
Ssm Zeiss Planar T	50	1,4	----	1200-1500
Zeiss Planar T*	85	1,4	----	1400-1500
Zeiss Sonnar T*	35	2,8	----	750-800
Zeiss Sonnar T*	55	1,8	----	900-1000
Zeiss Sonnar T*	135	1,8	----	1750-1900
Zeiss Sonnar T* Za	24-70	4	----	1000-1200
Zeiss Vario Sonnar T*	24	2	----	950-1250
Zeiss Vario-Sonnar T*	16-80	3,5-4,5	----	750-800
Zeiss Vario-Sonnar T* Ssm	24-70	2,8	----	1850-2300
Zeiss Vario-Sonnar T* Ssm	16-35	2,8	----	1000-1200

Staeble

Modello	Focale	f	Attacco	€
Choro	38	3,5	M39	100-120
Kata	45	2,8	----	25-45
Lineogon	35	3,5	M39	170-220
Staeble	50	4,8	----	550-650
Telexon	135	3,8	----	75-120
Telexon	90	5,6	----	90-120
Ultragon	210	8	----	25-45
Ultragon	150	8	----	25-45
Ultralit	50	2,8	----	100-140

Super Ozeck

Modello	Focale	f	Attacco	€
Super Ozeck	75-150	3,8	Canon	45-80
Super Ozeck	28	2,8	Pentax	45-70
Super Ozeck	135	2,8	Fujica-Ax	35-60
Super Ozeck	80-205	4,5	Canon Fd	25-45
Super Ozeck	80-200	5,5	Pentax K	22-45
Super Ozeck Auto Mc	35-150	3,5-4,5	Olympus Om	60- 85
Super Ozeck Mc Auto	38-70	3,5	----	40-70

Takumar

Modello	Focale	f	Attacco	€
Super Macro Takumar	50	4	M42	80-140
Super Mc	55	3,5	Pentax	120-160
Super Takumar	55	2	M42	35-55
Super Takumar	85	1,9	M42	190-250
Super Takumar	135	2,5	Pentax K	45-70
Super Takumar	150	4	M42	40-70

Super -Takumar	200	4	M42	35-60
Super Takumar Mc	35	3,5	M42	35-65
Super Takumar Mf	35	3,5	M42	45-65
Super-Takumar	55	1,8	M42	35-55
Super-Takumar	135	3,5	M42	29-45
Super-Takumar	50	1,4	M42	55-85
Super-Takumar	28	3,5	M42	45-70
Super-Takumar	135	3,5	M42	40-70
Takumar	28-80	3,5-4,5	Pentax	40-60
Takumar	135	2,5	Pentax K	35-60
Takumar	70-200	4	----	27-45
Takumar	24	3,5	M42	130-170
Takumar	400	5,6	M42	140-180
Takumar	28	3,5	M42	65-90
Takumar	80-200	4,5	----	70-100
Takumar	105	2,4	6x7	110-150
Takumar	135	3,5	M42	55-85
Takumar	105	2,8	M42	115-150
Takumar	300	4	M42	125-160
Takumar	18	11	M42	240-290
Takumar Auto	55	2,2	M42	65-90
Takumar Macro	28-80	3,5-4,5	Pentax	28-45
Takumar Macro Auto	28-80	3,5-4,5	----	50-80
Takumar Mc	35	2	M42	85-125
Takumar Mc	150	2,8	Pentax	70-100
Takumar Mc	300	4	M42	140-180
Takumar Mc	17	4	M42	160-210
Takumar Mc	85	1,9	M42	55-75
Takumar Smc Mf	200	4	Vite	100-140
Takumar Super Mc	105	2,8	----	90-120
Tele-Takumar	300	6,3	M42	75-100

Tamron

Modello	Focale	f	Attacco	€
Di Ii Pzd Vc	18-270	3,5-6,3	----	600-700
Di Ii Sp Macro	60	2	----	450-550
Di Ii Sp Macro	60	2	----	450-550
Di Ii Sp Xr Ld If	17-50	2,8	----	400-490
Di Ii Sp Xr Ld If Vc	17-50	2,8	----	500-600
Di Ii Sp Xr Ld If Vc	17-50	2,8	----	550-600
Di Ii Uw Ld If	10-24	3,5-4,5	----	550-650
Di Ii Uw Ld If	10-24	3,5-4,5	----	550-650
Di Ii Xr Ld If Macro	18-200	3,5-6,3	----	150-280
Di Iii Vc Af Dmf	18-200	3,5-6,3	Canon	500-600
Di Iii Vc Af Dmf	18-200	3,5-6,3	Sony-E	700-800
Di Ld Macro 1:2	70-300	4-5,6	----	150-220
Di Sp Ld If Macro	180	3,5	----	800-950
Di Sp Ld If Macro	70-200	2,8	----	850-950
Di Sp Ld If Macro	180	3,5	----	850-950
Di Sp Macro	90	2,8	----	550-620
Di Sp Macro 1:1	90	2,8	----	550-620
Di Sp Xr Ld If Macro	28-75	2,8	----	450-550
Di Usd Ld Xr If Vc	24-70	2,8	----	950-1200
Di Usd Xld Vc	70-300	4-5,6	----	450-520
Di Vc Usd	70-200	2,8	----	1600-1900
Pzd Vc Vxr	16-300	3,5-6,3	----	550-650
Pzd Vc Vxr	16-300	3,5-6,3	----	550-650
Sma Ld	14-150	3,5-5,8	Micro 4/3	500-600
Sma Ld	14-150	3,5-5,8	Micro 4/3	550-600
Sp Usd Vc Macro	90	2,8	----	600-700
Sp Usd Vc Macro	90	2,8	----	600-700

Sp Vc Usd	150-600	5-6,3	----	1200-1450
Ta mron	28-105	2,8	Nikon	140-180
Tamron	18-200	3,5-6,3	Nikon	150-250
Tamron	18-200	3,5-6,3	Eos	150-250
Tamron	24-70	3,3-5,6	Nikon	100-120
Tamron	18-270	3,5-6,3	Nikon	250-320
Tamron	70-300	4-5,6	Canon	180-250
Tamron	17-50	2,8	Canon	200-250
Tamron	70-300	4-5,6	Pentax	60-80
Tamron	500	8	Adaptal	140-180
Tamron	70-200	4,5	Olympus	25-50
Tamron	70-210	3,8-4	----	40-60
Tamron	80-210	3,8-4	Olympus	40-60
Tamron	28	2,5	Adaptall	50-90
Tamron	135	2,8	----	30-50
Tamron	35-135	3,5-4,2	----	60-90
Tamron Af	55-200	4-5,6	----	60-80
Tamron Macro	18-200	3,5-6,3	Pentax	140-170
Tamron Macro	80-210	3,8	K	80-100
Tamron Af	35-90	4,5-6	Pentax	80-120
Tamron Af	70-200	2,8	Pentax	400-500
Tamron Af Ld	200-400	5,6	Canon	180-200
Tamron Af Macro	70-300	4-5,6	Pentax	70-95
Tamron If Macro	28-300	3,5-6,3	Canon	180-240
Tamron Macro	70-300	4-5,6	Canon	90-150
Tamron Macro	70-150	3,5	----	40-60
Tamron Mc	35-135	3,5-4,5	----	60-90
Tamron Sp	90	2,5	Contax	140-180
Tamron Sp	70-300	4-5,6	Canon	260-320
Tamron St F	35-80	2,8-3,8	----	50-85
Vc Pzd Xr	28-300	3,5-6,3	----	800-950

Taylor & Hobson

Modello	Focale	f	Attacco	€
Anastigmat Series II	156	4,5	----	100-200
Apermax Projection	140	----	Projector	60-90
Cooke Portrait VI	460	5,6	----	450-550
Cooke Speed Panchro	18	1,7	----	450-600
Cooke Speed Panchro	18	1,7	T2	1200-1400
Cooke Speed Panchro	50	2	----	350-450
Cooke Speed Panchro	75	2	----	550-650
Cooke Speed Panchro	18	2	----	1000-1400
Ental	80	4,5	----	20-40
Filmo 70DL	24	1,9	C	350-450
Ivotal Anastigmat	48	1,4	----	400-500
Kinetal	75	2,6	C	550-650
Series VB ULF Anast	330	8	----	80-120
SerieX Anastigmat	156	2,5	----	1000-1400
Speed Panchro II	75	2	----	800-1000
Super Comat	35	1,9	----	25-50
Varotal T (cine)	40-400	4,5	----	900-1200
Vidital	80	1,5	C	350-450

Tefnon

Modello	Focale	f	Attacco	€
Ental	108	4,5	----	45-60
Tefnon	80-200	4	M42	20-30
Tefnon	28	2,8	Nikon Ai	28-45
Tefnon	28-85	3,5-4,5	Minolta	29-45
Tefnon	70-210	----	----	25-45
Tefnon Mc	80-200	4	Pentax	30-55
Tefnon Macro	75-205	3,8-4,8	Minolta	35-55
Tefnon Macro	28-200	3,8-5,6	Canon Fd	25-45
Tefnon Macro	28-80	3,8-4,8	----	25-45
Tefnon Macro	35-105	3,2-4	Pentax K	28-50
Tefnon Macro	70-162	3,5	----	30-60

Tiny Steinheil Cassar

Modello	Focale	f	Attacco	€
Tiny Steinheil cassar	36	3,5	D	25-35

Tokina

Modello	Focale	f	Attacco	€
Af At-X Af Dx	10 - 17	3,5-4,5	----	480-550
Af At-X D	80 - 400	4,5-5,6	----	550-650
Af At-X D Macro	100	2,8	----	290-380
Af At-X Pro Dx	16 - 50	2,8	----	550-620
Af At-X Pro Dx	50 - 135	2,8	----	550-620
Af At-X Pro Dx	12 - 24	4	----	450-540
Af At-X Dx Macro	35	2,8	----	380-440
Tokina	28-70	2,8	----	200-300
Tokina	80-200	4,5-5,6	Minolta	28-40
Tokina	28	2,8	Minolta	30-50
Tokina	20-35	3,5-4,5	----	250-290
Tokina Af	24-200	3,5-5,6	----	270-320
Tokina Af	20-35	3,5-4,5	Eos	180-240
Tokina Af At-X Dx	12-24	4	Canon	280-320
Tokina Dx At-X	16,5-135	3,5-5,6	Nikon	180-220
Tokina Sd Auto	70-210	4-5,6	----	50-70
TokinaAt-X Pro D	11-16	2,8	Nikon	400-450

Vega

Modello	Focale	f	Attacco	€
Vega7	20	2	M32	40-65
Vega-28B Mc	120	2,8	Kiev	150-200
Vega-22Y	103	5,6	Pe	60-85
Vega-12b	90	2,8	Kiev 60	80-110
Vega-11U	50	2,8	M39	70-100
Vega-9	50	2	Krasnogorsk	45-70
VEGA-5U	105	4	M42	24-45
Vega 11U	50	2,8	M39	15-25

Vivitar

Modello	Focale	f	Attacco	€
Macrofocusing	80-200	4,5	M42	20-30
Vivitar	28-70	3,5-4,8	Minolta	20-50
Vivitar	135	3,5	Nikon	35-55
Vivitar	70-210	3,5	Canon Fd	70-90
Vivitar	28-70	3,5-4,5	Minolta	28-48
Vivitar	28	2,8	Canon Fd	70-85
Vivitar	28	2,8	Minolta Md	60-90
Vivitar	70-210	4,5-5,6	Canon Fd	80-100
Vivitar	135	2,8	Canon	40-80
Vivitar	35-105	3,2-4	Canon	80-100
Vivitar	28	2,8	Pentax	30-60
Vivitar	35-105	3,2-4	Canon	50-90
Vivitar	135	2,8	Canon	40-80
Vivitar	70-210	4,5-5,6	Yashica	40-60
Vivitar	28-80	3,5-5,6	----	40-70
Vivitar	19	3,8	Canon Fd	80-120
Vivitar	28	2,8	Pentax K	30-50
Vivitar	28	2,8	Olympus Om	20-40
Vivitar Macro	75-300	4,5-5,6	Pentax	30-60
Vivitar Macro	70-300	4,2-5,8	----	50-70
Vivitar Macro	70-210	4,5-5,6	----	28-50
Vivitar Serie 1	70-210	2,8-4	----	55-80
Vivitar Serie1	70-210	3,5	----	55-80

Voigtlander

Modello	Focale	f	Attacco	€
Apo Lanthar	210	4,5	----	1400-1800
Apo-Lanthar	180	4	Pentax	700-800
Color-Heliar	75	2,5	----	190-240
Color-Skopar	21	4	Leica M	190-250
Color-Skopar	35	2,5	----	140-180
Color-Skopar As	28	2,8	Canon	270-320

Color-Ultron	50	1,8	----	25-45
Dynaret	100	4,8	Vitessa T	70-100
Heliar SuperWide As	15	4,5	Leica	260-300
Heliar Ultra Wide	12	5,6	Leica M	280-350
Lanthar Sl Apo	90	3,5	Nikon	360-400
Nokton	40	1,4	Leica M	190-240
Nokton	35	1,2	Leica M	680-750
Nokton	25	0,95	4/3	350-400
Nokton	50	1,1	Leica M	450-550
Nokton As	35	1,2	Leica	450-550
Nokton Asp argento	50	1,5	Leica	290-350
Nokton Classic	35	1,4	Leica M	290-390
Skopar	28	3,5	----	250-290
Snapshot Skopar	25	4	----	180-260
Super-Wide Heliar	15	4,5	Leica	180-240
Ultragon	19-35	3,5-4,5	Minolta	50-80
Ultron	35	1,7	Leica	220-280
Ultron	35	1,7	Leica	200-250
Voigtlander	50	2	----	150-250
Voigtlander Lanthar	150	4,5	----	400-600
Voigtlander Dynarex	200	3,5	----	90-140
Voigtlander Heliar	75	2,5	Nikon	270-320
Voigtlander Zoomar	36-82	2,8	----	800-950

Voigtlander & Sohn

Modello	Focale	f	Attacco	€
Euryskop	190	10,5	----	400-500
Agb Heliar	300	4,5	----	220-280
Collinear Ii	----	----	----	1800-2400
Euryscop Iv	----	----	----	2800-3100
Euryscop Iii (1889)	----	----	----	2000-3000
Euryscop Portrait	----	----	----	950-1100

Volna

Modello	Focale	f	Attacco	€
Volna	90	2,8	Vite 42	140-180
Volna MC	50	1,8	Pentax	80-120
Volna-3 MC	80	2,8	Kiev	55-80
Volna-9 MC Macro	50	2,8	M42	90-150
Volna-9 MC Macro	50	2	----	80-120

Xarkov

Modello	Focale	f	Attacco	€
Upp	55	2,8	----	15-28

Yashica

Modello	Focale	f	Attacco	€
Yashica	50	1,9	Contax	28-42
Yashica	135	2,8	Contax-	40-60
Yashica	28-80	3,9-4,9	Contax-	40-50
Yashica	35-70	3,5-4,5	Contax	50-80
Yashica	135	2,8	----	50-80
Yashica	50	2	----	30-50
Yashica	50	1,4	Yashica	90-120
Yashica Af	28-70	3,5-4,5	----	45-65
Yashica Af	70-200	4,5-6	----	40-60
Yashica Af	70-210	4,5	----	35-55
Yashica Af	50	1,8	----	45-60
Yashica Af Macro	60	2,8	Yashica	100-140
Yashica Af Macro	35-70	3,3-4,5	----	28-45
Yashica Af Macro	60	2,8	----	150-170
Yashica Dsb	28	2,8	Contax	75-100
Yashica Dsb	35-105	3,8-4,8	Contax	55-80
Yashica Dsb	55	1,2	Contax	25-45

Yashica Dsb	135	2,8	Contax	55-80
Yashica Dsb	38-90	3,5	Contax	70-110
Yashica Dsb	55	2	Contax	25-45
Yashica Dsb	70-210	4	----	80-100
Yashica Dsb	70-180	4,5	----	85-100
Yashica Mc Macro	75-200	4,5	Yashica	60-90
Yashica Ml	42-75	3,5-4,5	----	40-65
Yashica Ml	35	2	----	110-140
Yashica Ml	24	2,8	----	150-250
Yashica Ml	15	2,8	----	600-800
Yashica Ml	28-210	3,8-4,8	Contax	120-160
Yashica Ml Macro	28-85	3,5-4,5	----	200-270
Yashica Ml Macro	100	4	----	140-180
Yashinon Auto	55	1,8	M42	45-75
Yashinon Ds	50	1,7	M42	45-70

Yvar

Modello	Focale	f	Attacco	€
Bolex H16 Macro	150	3,3	C	1100-1400
Bolex Yvar	13	1,9	----	29-45
Bolex Yvar	100	3,3	C	400-500
Kern Paillard	12,5	2,8	D	150-250
Kern Paillard Yvar	15	2,8	C	50-80
Kern Paillard Yvar	75	2,8	C	250-290
Kern Yvar	150	4	----	150-200
Yvar	13	1,8	D	45-70
Yvar	12,5	2,5	D	29-45

Will Wetzlar

Modello	Focale	f	Attacco	€
Maginon	85	2,8	Projector	28-45
Maginon	150	3	Projector	28-45
Maginon	100	2,8	Projector	40-65
Maginon	50	2,8	----	25-40

Stellar	85	2,8	Projector	25-40
Super Paxigon	200	3,5	Projector	28-45
Vario Stellar	95	2,8	----	250-350
Vario Travenon	16,5-30	1,5	Projector	28-45
Wetzlar	70-210	3,5	Projector	28-60
Wetzlar	20-52	1,5	Projector	25-40
Wilon	75	4,5	----	25-40
Wilon	50	3,5	Pe	25-40

Wollensak

Modello	Focale	f	Attacco	€
Wollensak (1900 brass)	----	8	----	600-700

Zeiss e Carl Zeiss

Modello	Focale	f	Attacco	€
Apochromat W	70	2,5	----	80-120
Biogon	21	2,8	----	1000-1200
Biogon ZM	25	2,8	----	1000-1200
Biogon ZM	28	2,8	----	1000-1100
Biogon ZM	35	2	----	1000-1200
Carl Zeiss Biogon	21	2,8	Leica M	1200-1400
Carl Zeiss Biogon argento/nero	25	2,8	Leica M	1000-1250
Carl Zeiss Biogon argento/nero	28	2,8	Leica M	950-1100
Carl Zeiss Biogon argento/nero	35	2	Leica M	950-1250
Carl Zeiss Biogon argento/nero	35	2,8	Leica M	750-950
Carl Zeiss C Sonnar argento/nero	50	1,5	Leica M	1100-1300

Carl Zeiss Distagon	18	4	Leica M	1000-1500
C. Zeiss Tele Tessar nero	85	4	Leica M	800-900
Carl Zeiss Tessar	45	2,8	Vite 42	150-200
C-Sonnar ZM	50	1,5	----	900-1200
Distagon ZF2	15	2,8	----	2600-2800
Distagon ZF2	35	1,4	----	1650-1800
Jena Flektogon	20	4	Exakta	210-240
Jena Anast (1900 ottone)	360	6,3	----	1000-2000
Jena Biotar	58	2	Exakta	220-260
Jena Tessar T	50	2,8	Exakta	140-180
Loxia	35	2	----	1100-1250
Loxia	50	2	----	800-950
Milvus	21	2,8	----	1600-1750
Milvus	35	2	----	950-1100
Milvus	50	1,4	----	1100-1200
Milvus	85	1,4	----	1600-1800
Milvus Macro	50	2	----	1000-1200
Milvus Macro	100	2	----	1550-1750
Otus	55	1,4	----	2800-3500
Otus	85	1,4	----	3800-4400
Planar T* ZF2	50	1,4	----	600-700
Planar ZM	50	2	----	750-850
Touit	12	2,8	----	960-1100
Touit	32	1,8	----	650-780
Zeiss Distagon	15	2,8	Canon-Nikon	2500-2900
Zeiss Distagon	35	1,4	----	700-800
Zeiss Distagon	28	2,8	----	270-340
Zeiss Distagon T	18	3,5	Canon-Nikon	1000-1400
Zeiss Distagon T	21	2,8	Canon-Nikon	1500-2000
Zeiss Distagon T	28	2	Canon-Nikon	1000-1400
Zeiss Distagon T	35	2	Canon-Nikon	950-1100
Zeiss Loxia	35	2	Sony	1000-1250

Zeiss Planar T	50	2	Canon-Nikon	1000-1400
Zeiss Planar T	100	2	Canon-Nikon	1500-1900
Zeiss Planar T	85	1,4	Canon-Nikon	950-1400
Zeiss Sonnar	135	2,8	----	170-220
Zeiss Sonnar	28-70	3,5-4,5	----	200-300
Zeiss Tessar	45	2,8	Contax	150-220

Zenitar

Modello	Focale	f	Attacco	€
Fisheye	16	2,8	Samsung NX	160-220
Fisheye	16	2,8	Canon FD	160-220
Zenitar	50	2	Olympus 4/3	70-100
Zenitar	50	2	Sony Nex	45-70
Zenitar	50	2	Minolta MD	70-95
Zenitar	50	2	Contax/Yashica	70-95
Zenitar	50	2	M42	40-60
Zenitar S	50	1,2	Canon EOS	350-450
Zenitar-C	16	2,8	Canon	170-220
Zenitar-C	16	2,8	Sony Alpha	180-240
Zenitar-C	16	2,8	M42	180-240

Zenith

Modello	Focale	f	Attacco	€
Helios	58	2	Zenith	25-50
Helios 44 argento 1955	58	2	M39	50-80
Helios M 42	58	2	M42	25-45
Zenith	50	1,8	Minolta Md	25-45
Zenith Mc-Mir	20	3,5	M42	120-160

Zenza Bronica

Modello	Focale	f	Attacco	€
Zenzanon	150	3,5	----	80-120
Zenzanon	75	2,8	----	50-75
Zenzanon	100	2,8	----	150-190
Zenzanon E	150	3,5	----	100-140
Zenzanon E	100	4	----	200-280
Zenzanon Mc	200	4	----	180-220
Zenzanon Mc	200	4,5	----	160-200
Zenzanon Mc	40	4	----	160-200
Zenzanon Mc	50	2,8	----	170-220
Zenzanon Mc	250	5,6	----	170-220
Zenzanon Pe	40	4	----	500-600
Zenzanon Pe	60	2,8	----	350-450
Zenzanon Pe	180	4,5	----	400-480
Zenzanon Pe	75	2,8	----	120-160
Zenzanon Pe	135	4	----	350-420
Zenzanon Pe	180	4,5	----	45-80
Zenzanon Pe	45-90	4-5,6	----	210-270
Zenzanon Pg	100	3,5	----	170-240
Zenzanon Ps	150	4	----	140-180
Zenzanon Ps	200	4,5	----	150-190
Zenzanon Ps	65	4	----	200-250
Zenzanon Ps	50	3,5	----	250-290
Zenzanon Ps Asp	50-100	4,5	----	500-600
Zenzanon Ps Macro	110	4	----	250-300
Zenzanon Rf	45	4	----	450-500
Zenzanon S	80	2,8	----	70-95
Zenzanon S	50	3,5	----	100-150
Zenzanon S	80	2,8	----	55-80
Zenzanon S	105	3,5	----	140-190
Zenzanon S	250	5,6	----	120-150
Zenzanon S	500	8	----	600-700

Altri lavori pubblicati dall'autore

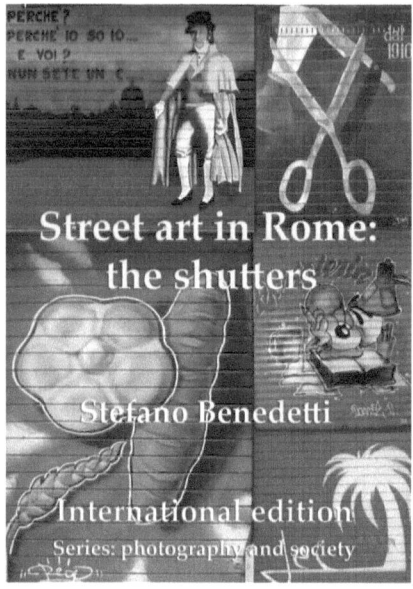

Questo libro è un tributo a Roma che è un museo a cielo aperto che, oltre ad esporre i monumenti, mostra migliaia di opere artistiche realizzate sulle saracinesche dei negozi. Opere che i tradizionali circuiti turistici non mostrano.

Nel libro sono raccolte oltre duecento opere tra le più belle e significative. Il libro è scritto nel linguaggio fotografico supportato da traduzioni in inglese laddove nelle immagini ci siano rappresentati testi in italiano

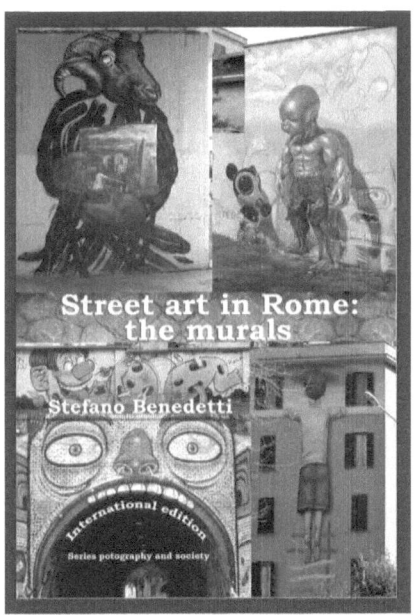

Il libro è scritto, come dice l'autore, nell'unico linguaggio comprensibile in tutto il mondo: la fotografia. Le immagini sono supportate dalla traduzione in lingua inglese quando ci sono rappresentate scritte in lingua italiana o laddove nel libro è necessario fornire indicazioni. Infatti i murales sono divisi per quartiere o zona di Roma e per ognuna è fornita una mappa e le indicazioni per raggiungerla con i mezzi pubblici. Nel libro ci sono oltre 260 opere tra le più belle e significative che potete vedere a Roma.

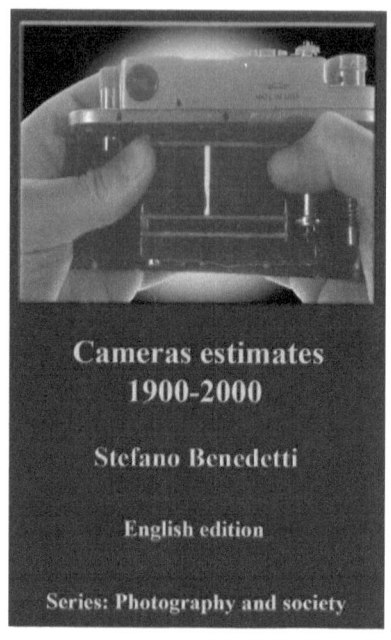

Cameras estimates
1900-2000

Stefano Benedetti

English edition

Series: Photography and society

A useful book to the collector, the amateur photographer, the antique dealer and the seller of cameras. In the book there are 2,200 assessments of cameras ordered alphabetically by manufacturer name. From index of the book you can go directly to the brand of interest.

Estimates are based on hundreds of thousands of offers in the market of antique cameras detected in Europe, America and Asia.

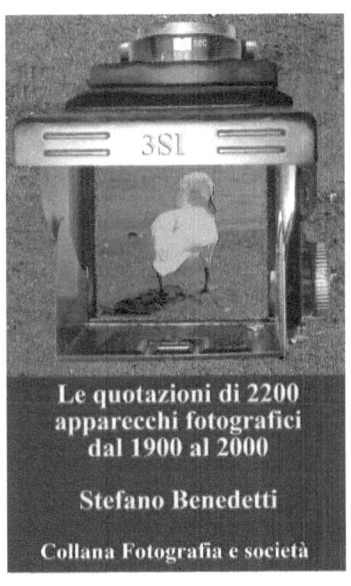

Versione in lingua italiana di Cameras estimates 1900-2000. Il libro contiene oltre 2200 stime di fotocamere ordinate alfabeticamente secondo il marchio. Le stime sono basate su una lunga indagine condotta in Italia, Europa, America e Asia volta a determinare una valutazione media dell'apparecchio. Dall'indice si accede direttamente al marchio che interessa. Insieme a questo libro che avete letto, risulta una guida utile e indispensabile per i collezionisti, gli antiquari e i rivenditori di materiale fotografico.

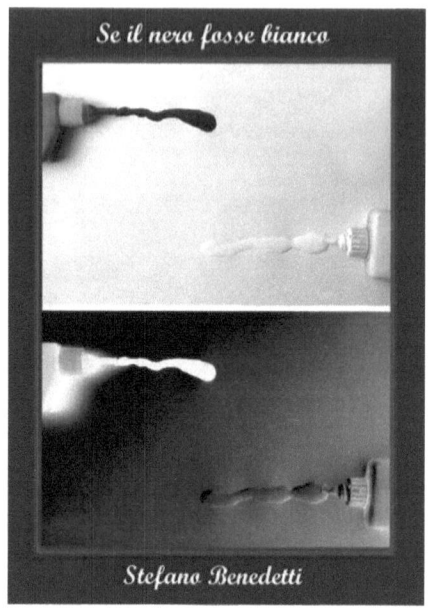

Un libro, unico nel suo genere, che spiega la sintassi e la composizione del linguaggio fotografico. L'esposizione è supportata da centinaia di fotografie, disegni, schemi e risulta chiara ed accessibile da chiunque. Gli argomenti trattati sono molteplici e investono quasi tutti i campi della fotografia amatoriale e professionale. L'autore è un fotografo professionista con decenni d'attività che, nel tempo, gli hanno permesso di delineare un insieme di regole sintattiche e metodi di composizione.

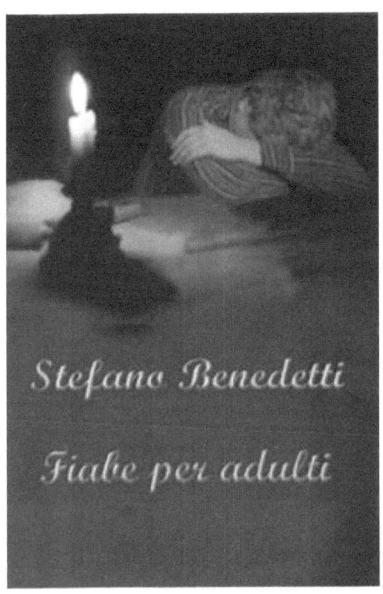

Fiabe per adulti perchè i bambini hanno fantasia per crearle da soli. Il libro è una raccolta di fiabe che trasportano in mondi fantastici evocando nel lettore sensazioni che vanno al di la delle pagine scritte. Le tecniche usate sono diverse: si va dalla fiaba breve a quelle più lunghe ma tutte hanno la prerogativa di far riflettere sognando ad occhi aperti.

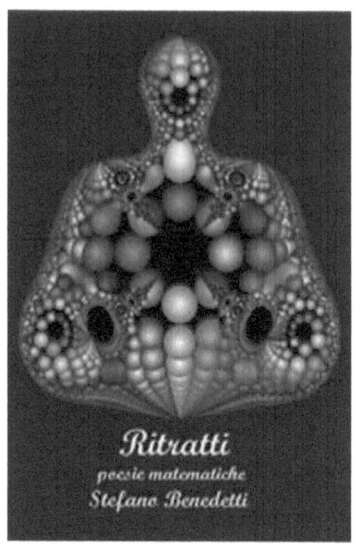

Godere della poesia, vivere la matematica. Il libro è composto da due parti. La prima è una raccolta di poesie che delineano ritratti di persone e di vita quotidiana. La seconda parte introduce il lettore, in modo semplice e chiaro, ai metodi di analisi matematica dei testi letterari utilizzando le poesie del libro. I metodi di analisi, introdotti dall'autore, sono innovativi e non sono delle mere statistiche, ma si basano sulle proprietà intrinseche dell'alfabeto e del vocabolario di riferimento.

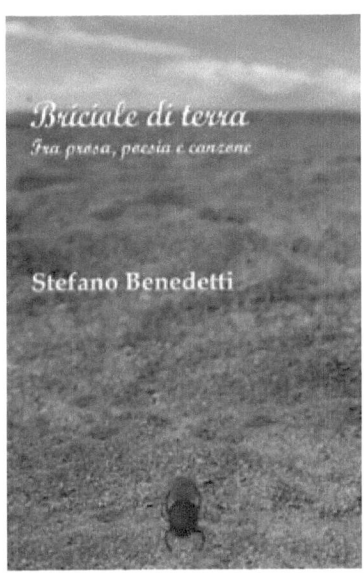

Briciole di terra
Fra prosa, poesia e canzone

Stefano Benedetti

Le parole sono come le briciole di terra che, finché restano sparse, sono desiderio solo di piccole creature, ma quando ben si amalgamano diventano campagne, valli, montagne, pianeti, universi. Una raccolta di scritti inediti che spaziano fra poesia, prosa e canzone.

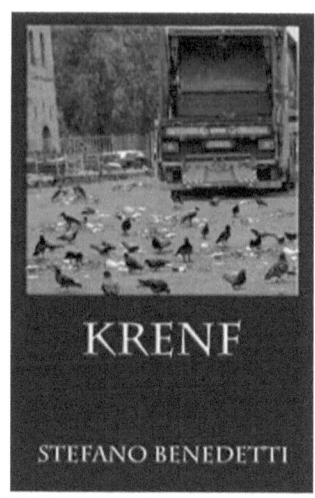

Krenf è morto. Un libro dedicato alla sua vita nel quartiere latino a Roma dove per tanti anni ha vissuto. Krenf racconta, parla di se, dei suoi amici, dei suoi nemici, dei suoi pregiudizi razziali, delle sue idiosincrasie, dei suoi deliri religiosi, della rabbia che lo ha sempre animato rendendolo violento, arrogante, superbo. Un Krenf reale, diverso dalle sue eleganti apparenze, dalle sue garbate movenze, da quell'immagine stereotipata che hanno tutti coloro che non l'hanno conosciuto...

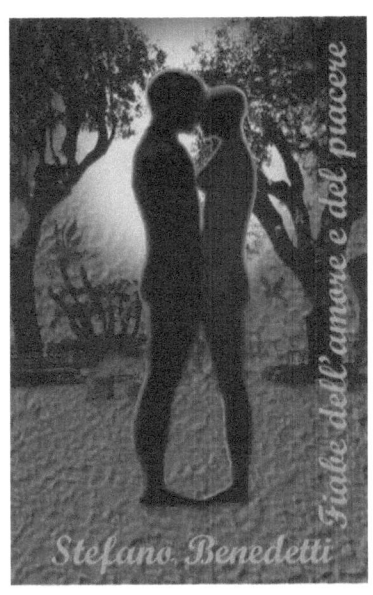

Fiabe dell'amore e del piacere

Stefano Benedetti

Parlare dell'amore e del piacere senza trascendere nell'accademico o invischiandosi in pornografia inutile, è impresa difficile. Sopratutto perché ognuno di noi in fondo, in fondo, ha dei preconcetti che non gli consentono di valutare in maniera totalmente obiettiva. Qualcuno leggendo questo titolo ha pensato ad un contenuto a luci rosse e mi ha chiesto se questo libro fosse adatto a tutte le età. La cosa certa è che ho provato a parlarne in maniera serena e sana senza sacrificare la verità. e.

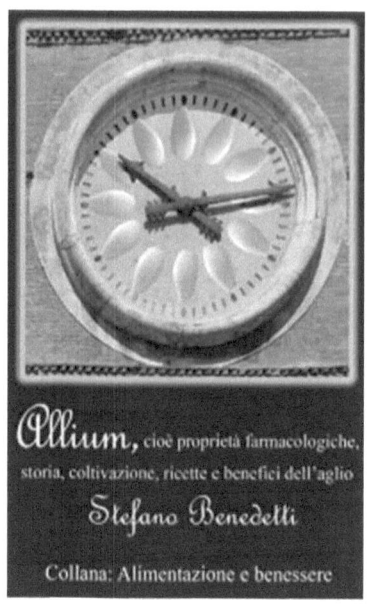

Il primo libro della collana Alimentazione e benessere dedicato all'aglio. Il libro parte dalla presenza di questo prezioso alimento nella storia e nella letteratura per poi passare alle sue importanti proprietà farmacologiche. Altri parti del libro forniscono informazioni sulla coltivazione della pianta e su come impiegarlo in cucina fornendo utili e dettagliate ricette di preparazione. Ci sono poi sezioni che integrano, nel quadro generale, informazioni varie siano esse di carattere scientifico o semplici curiosità sull'aglio. Il libro è scritto in maniera chiara, lineare e se c'è necessità di usare termini non comuni, questi sono spiegati.

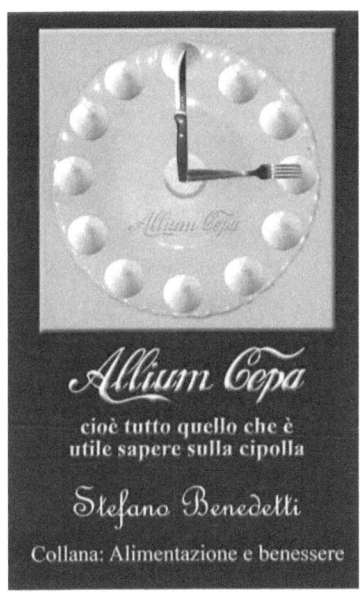

Allium Cepa
cioè tutto quello che è
utile sapere sulla cipolla

Stefano Benedetti

Collana: Alimentazione e benessere

Il secondo volume della collana Alimentazione e benessere dedicato alla cipolla. Questo prezioso bulbo dalle molteplici proprietà farmacologiche è anche alimento diffuso e apprezzato in tutto il mondo. Il libro è una ricca fonte di informazioni: dalla sua presenza nella storia umana a quella nella letteratura, dalle proprietà farmacologiche ai metodi di assunzione per fini terapeutici, dalle ricette culinarie alle sagre dedicate alla cipolla, dai metodi di coltivazione alle malattie che possono colpire la pianta. Altri settori integrano questa visione globale su uno dei prodotti della terra davvero indispensabili per il benessere umano.

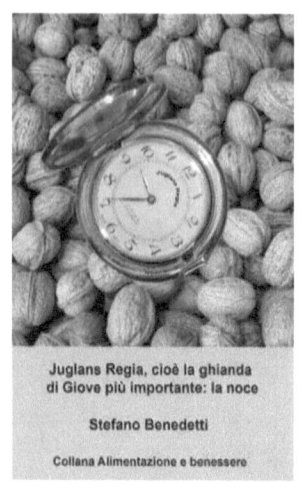

Juglans Regia, cioè la ghianda
di Giove più importante: la noce

Stefano Benedetti

Collana Alimentazione e benessere

Il terzo volume della collana Alimentazione e benessere
dedicato alla noce. In questo volume sono esplorati tutti gli
aspetti di questo importante frutto che contiene sostanze
favorevoli al benessere del corpo e che è molto apprezzato
dal punto di vista culinario. Il libro parte da una desrizione
dell'albero per poi cercare le tracce della noce nella storia e
nella letteratura umana. Quindi riporta i miti, le leggende e
le superstizioni che hanno e che ancora circondano la noce.
Non sono certo trascurati gli aspetti fitoterapici e benefici
della noce così come non è trascurata la coltivazione. Le
informazioni che potete trovare sono di molteplici generi:
ricette, sagre e fiere, presenza negli stemmi comuanali e
delle famiglie, proverbi e modi di dire, la noce in tutte le
lingue del mondo, varietà del noce e giochi antichi e
attuali. Insomma un viaggio nel mondo della noce da non
perdere.

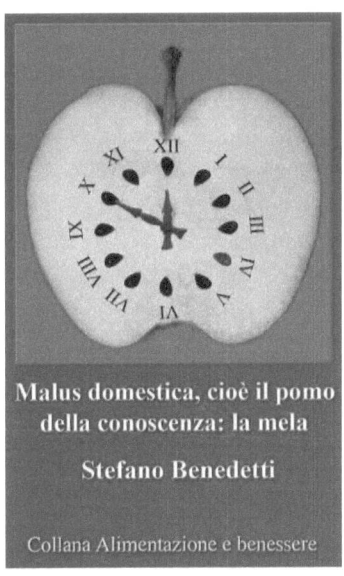

Malus domestica, cioè il pomo della conoscenza: la mela

Stefano Benedetti

Collana Alimentazione e benessere

Il quarto volume della collana Alimentazione e benessere dedicato alla mela. Un libro prezioso che esplora tutti gli aspetti di questo splendido frutto così importante per il benessere umano. Si parla della coltivazione dell'albero, delle proprietà fitoterapiche del frutto, delle tracce nella storia e nell'arte umana, delle molteplici varietà e di tante altre cose che direttamente o indirettamente riguardano il melo. Un libro da non perdere che va ad arricchire questa splendida collana.

Chi distribuisce i libri

La versione stampata	
Street art in Rome: the shutters	Create Space-Amazon
Street art in Rome: the murals	Create Space-Amazon
Cameras estimates 1900-2000	Createspace-Amazon
Se il nero fosse bianco	Feltrinelli - Ilmiolibro
Fiabe per adulti	Feltrinelli - Ilmiolibro
Briciole di terra	Feltrinelli - Ilmiolibro
Ritratti, poesie matematiche	Feltrinelli - Ilmiolibro
Fiabe dell'amore e del piacere	Feltrinelli - Ilmiolibro
Krenf	Feltrinelli - Ilmiolibro
Allium, cioè proprietà farmacologiche, storia, coltivazione, ricette e benefici dell'aglio	Create Space-Amazon
Allium Cepa, cioè tutto quello che è utile sapere sulla cipolla	Create Space-Amazon
Juglan Regia, cioè la ghianda più importanta di Giove: la noce	Create Space-Amazon
Malus Domestica, cioè il pomo della conoscenza: la mela	Create Space-Amazon
Le quotazioni di 2200 apparecchi fotografici dal 1900 al 2000	Create Space-Amazon

La versione ebook	
Street art in Rome: the shutters	Create Space-Amazon–Kobo-Feltrinelli-Mondadori
Street art in Rome: the murals	Create Space-Amazon–Kobo-Feltrinelli-Mondadori
Cameras estimates 1900-2000	Create Space–Amazon–Kobo-Feltrinelli-Mondadori
Se il nero fosse bianco	Feltrinelli–Ilmiolibro–Amazon-Kobo Mondadori–Rizzoli–Hoepli-Unilibro Ultimabook–Ibs–Unità- Bookrepublic

Fiabe per adulti	Feltrinelli–Ilmiolibro–Amazon-Kobo Mondadori–Rizzoli–Hoepli–Unilibro Ultimabook–Ibs–Bookrepublic-Unità
Briciole di terra	Feltrinelli–Ilmiolibro–Amazon-Kobo Mondadori–Rizzoli–Hoepli–Unilibro Ultimabook–Ibs–Bookrepublic-Unità
Ritratti, poesie matematiche	Feltrinelli–Ilmiolibro–Amazon-Kobo Mondadori–Rizzoli–Hoepli–Unilibro Ultimabook–Ibs–Bookrepublic-Unità
Fiabe dell'amore e del piacere	Feltrinelli–Ilmiolibro–Amazon-Kobo Mondadori–Rizzoli–Hoepli–Unilibro Ultimabook–Ibs–Bookrepublic-Unità
Krenf	Feltrinelli–Ilmiolibro–Amazon-Kobo Mondadori–Rizzoli–Hoepli–Unilibro Ultimabook–Ibs–Bookrepublic-Unità
Allium, cioè proprietà farmacologiche, storia, coltivazione, ricette e benefici dell'aglio	Create Space-Kobo-Amazon-Feltrinelli-Mondadori
Allium Cepa, cioè tutto quello che è utile sapere sulla cipolla	Create Space-Kobo-Amazon-Feltrinelli-Mondadori
Juglan Regia, cioè la ghianda più importante di Giove: la noce	Create Space-Kobo-Amazon-Feltrinelli-Mondadori
Malus Domestica, cioè il pomo della conoscenza: la mela	Create Space-Kobo-Amazon-Feltrinelli-Mondadori
Le quotazioni di 2200 apparecchi fotografici dal 1900 al 2000	Create Space-Kobo-Amazon-Feltrinelli-Mondadori

Contatta l'autore

Se vuoi contattare l'autore per un commento, una critica, per conoscerlo o qualsiasi cosa che ritieni utile e necessaria, puoi scrivere all'indirizzo email: **arte@systemeuro.com**

www.ingramcontent.com/pod-product-compliance
Lightning Source LLC
Chambersburg PA
CBHW030853180526
45163CB00004B/1557